MW01673067

Winning Badminton

By James L. Breen, Ph.D.
and
Donald C. Paup, Ph.D.

A Championship Player
National Instructor
National Coach

Published By:
THE ATHLETIC INSTITUTE
200 Castlewood Drive
North Palm Beach, FL 33408
U.S.A.

Copyright © 1983 by The Athletic Institute

All rights reserved
including the right of reproduction
in whole or in part in any form.
Published by The Athletic Institute
200 Castlewood Drive
North Palm Beach, Florida 33408
Printed in the United States of America

Library of Congress Catalog Card Number 82-7432
ISBN O-8760-068-7

A WORD FROM THE PUBLISHER

THIS SPORTS PUBLICATION, is but one item in a comprehensive list of sports instructional aids, such as video cassettes, 16mm films, 8mm silent loops and filmstrips which are made available by The Athletic Institute. This book is part of a master plan which seeks to make the benefits of athletics, physical education and recreation available to everyone.

The Athletic Institute is a not-for-profit organization devoted to the advancement of athletics, physical education and recreation. The Institute believes that participation in athletics and recreation has benefits of inestimable value to the individual and to the community.

The nature and scope of the many Institute programs are determined by a Professional Advisory Committee, whose members are noted for their outstanding knowledge, experience and ability in the fields of athletics, physical education and recreation.

The Institute believes that through this book the reader will become a better performer, skilled in the fundamentals of this fine event. Knowledge and the practice necessary to mold knowledge into playing ability are the keys to real enjoyment in playing any game or sport.

Howard J. Bruns
President and Chief Executive Officer
The Athletic Institute

Dustin A Cole
Executive Director
The Athletic Institute

TABLE OF CONTENTS

KEY TO DIAGRAMS

Solid Circle — Base
Empty Circle — Player Position
S — Smasher, attacker or server
F — Forecourt player
D — Defender
R — Receiver
P — Partner

In doubles diagrams:
M — Male
F — Female

INTRODUCTION

INTRODUCTION

Badminton offers fun and fitness for everyone. It is a sport that is easily learned but difficult to master. A beginning player receives pleasure and exercise immediately; and yet at the same time an advanced player can get a vigorous workout by playing just one game. Research studies of movement show that a badminton player uses more arm action in one game than the average baseball pitcher does in a nine-inning baseball game. Too, a top-flight badminton player runs farther in one game than a running back or end does in a sixty-minute football game.

Badminton is a game played by women, men and children. Thus, it is often called a family sport. Adaptation to small areas, indoors and outdoors, at a minimum cost provides an opportunity for everyone to participate. The perimeter of badminton includes the opportunity for the physically handicapped to participate with each other on an equal basis. As one develops advanced skills and desires competition, either team or individual, the opportunity for tournament play is available in almost any geographical section of the United States. Tournaments sponsored by local badminton clubs (there are over 300) sanctioned by the U.S. Badminton Association provide tournament competition for all age groups from 13 years and under, to 60 years and over, in Ladies' Singles, Men's Singles, Ladies' Doubles, Men's Doubles and Mixed Doubles events.

Physiological Benefits: Moderate to vigorous exercise can be experienced. It is a rhythmic game of running, jumping, stretching, starting, stopping, and twisting which contributes to the development of several fitness components, such as agility, flexibility, balance, endurance and the maintenance of muscle tone. Research studies give evidence that badminton is one of the sports that contributes to the efficiency of the cardio-vascular system. (The rhythmic movement employed produces the contraction and relaxation of the muscles which delivers a more efficient pumping of the blood within the circulatory system).

Psychological Benefits: The human organism is continually seeking "ego"-satisfying experiences. Badminton, which is lifetime in scope, gives opportunity to the "play" concept which is a part of these pleasurable experiences. The concept of "play" in infancy and early childhood is that experience which is pleasurable. Through badminton, the adult can experience the "play" concept which can give periods of elation as opposed to depression, consequently advancing better mental health. "Aging" in man's mind is often brought to focus when it is said, "You are too old to do this and that." Badminton is that sport which can defy this type of reasoning, since a relatively high level of achievement can be experienced at any age.

In addition, emotional tensions can be released through vigorous physical activity. According to psychologists, the outward expression of hostile feelings is a healthy therapeutic process. Badminton provides a climate, socially accepted, in which to vent these feelings. Subconscious release of these hostile feelings may be realized by SMASHING a shuttle.

Sportsmanship, courtesies, and self-discipline are concomitant learnings of a well-played badminton game.

Sociological Benefits: Gathering of groups is a social integration which is fundamental to life. Many segments of society are brought together through badminton clubs in the United States. Many tournaments are held each year by these clubs, thus providing additional opportunities for competition and social gatherings. Since badminton is suited for male and female, young and old, family participation is very popular. While participants in most racket sports pre-arrange their partners and schedule a specified court time, club play in badminton offers a unique opportunity for socialization. Badminton players generally arrive at a playing site for an evening of play. They make up games as the players arrive and change partners and opponents for singles, doubles, and mixed doubles several times during the course of the evening.

Extra-Political Benefits: Badminton participation encompasses the world. With international competition in badminton being a common denominator, there is at least hope for a better political understanding; like art, music, and literature, badminton is aesthetically understood. A well-executed drop shot is appreciated even though there exists a political and language barrier.

The national gross product of any country is its people. Participants, not spectators, is the aim of a lifetime sport. Badminton can play a major role in this endeavor since it is a fun sport that can be played by everyone.

BRIEF HISTORY

There is some question as to the origin of the sport of badminton; however, there is evidence that a game similar to badminton was played in China some centuries ago, and there is mention of the game as far back as the twelfth century. In the Royal Court records of England, a portrait "Young Prince Sulkonsik" by Adam Mangohi, who lived about 1700, shows young members of the royal family of Poland holding a shuttlecock and racket with a position similar to that used by modern players preparing to serve. A portrait by Jean Simeon Chardin (1699-1779) depicts a young girl with a racket and shuttle. This portrait today hangs in the Uffizi Gallery in Florence, Italy. There is a steel engraving "Children Playing Badminton," France 1805, which is displayed in the Basel Sports Museum in Switzerland. These records of history make no mention of the court used for badminton; however, the first rules of the game published in book form by Massey in 1877 illustrated the court shaped like an "hour-glass." In subsequent rules in 1901, the court was changed to the rectangular court as we know it today.

It is generally accepted that the modern game of badminton was named when some British Army officers home on leave from India played the game at Badminton, the country estate of the Duke of Beaufort in Gloucestershire, England. This game was called "Poona" in India. The date was sometime around 1873. It is assumed that the game was played on the "hour-glass court" since this shape of court was depicted in the rule book until 1901.

In 1879 the New York Badminton Club was founded. This is said to be the oldest organized club in the world. Original records stored in the New York City Museum of History substantiate this claim. The English Badminton Association is believed to have been founded in 1893. This, according to record, was the first association in badminton. The second organized badminton association was founded in Ireland in 1899. This organization was the founding member of the International Badminton Federation (IBF) in 1934. The "American Badminton Association" (ABA) was founded in 1936. However, in 1977, the ABA changed its name to the "United States Badminton Association (USBA)."

The first international badminton competition was played in 1903 in Dublin, Ireland, between English and Irish teams. It was not until 1934 that the IBF organized international competition which included nine national badminton organizations. By 1939 the numbers had risen to 15 and today there are 53 countries participating in international competition.

As recently as 1977 another international badminton organization was founded and was called the World Badminton Federation (WBF). The first WBF championship was held in Malmo, Sweden in 1977, with thirty countries sending players to the event.

The IBF is the regulatory body for international cup events known as the Uber Cup for women's competition and the Thomas Cup for men. Both of these events are contested every three years. The Thomas Cup competition was started in 1948 and has been won by Malaysia or Indonesia each time. The Uber Cup competition was initiated in 1956. The U.S. won the first 3 championships and Japan and Indonesia the most recent. In 1982 the IBF changed the Uber and Thomas Cup format to biennial competition with a World Championship event being held in the alternate year.

The oldest and most prestigious of all international competition is the All-England Championship which was started back in 1899 and is held annually. The winner of this event has generally been considered the world badminton champion.

In 1976 the Pan American Confederation was formed, including the U.S., Canada, Jamaica, Mexico and Peru, to provide team competition every three years for these countries. Due to financial and organizational considerations, the U.S. withdrew from the Pan American Confederation in 1980.

In April, 1966, the first full international competition, later to be known as the Devlin Cup, was contested between Canada and the U.S. in Concord, New Hampshire. This competition was replaced by the Pan American Games competition in 1977. However, since the U.S. pulled out of the Pan American Confederation the Devlin Cup event was resumed in 1980. This competition is held every three years, alternating with the Thomas Cup and Uber Cup contests.

In 1981 the First World Games were held in San Jose, California. Badminton was one of the events featured in these games. This event was significant in that this was the first time players from the People's Republic of China have competed against other world class players in tournament competition. The Chinese won four of the five events.

In 1975 badminton made a stab at commercialism when the Canadian Badminton Association conducted the first-ever large prize money event — a $19,000 tournament. Afterward the IBF passed new regulations limiting prizes to $200 per event. Since that time international badminton has been an entirely amateur game. By keeping the game amateur the IBF thought that badminton could become an Olympic event. Badminton was presented as a demonstration sport at the 1972 Olympic Games in Munich, Germany.

The IBF in 1979 approved for the first time in the history of the sport open-professional badminton. This action by the IBF was to give badminton players an opportunity to negotiate professional contracts. By doing this, more attention would be given the sport and, hence, provide better opportunity to get the sport into the Olympics.

In 1969 the first intercollegiate badminton tournament was held for women in New Orleans, Louisiana. This tournament has been held annually and is now sponsored by the AIAW (Association for Intercollegiate Athletics for Women). The first men's intercollegiate tournament was held in Toledo, Ohio in 1975, and was sponsored by the Athletic Institute and the American Alliance for Health, Physical Education, Recreation and Dance.

Figure 1 lists important dates and events in the history of badminton.

IMPORTANT BADMINTON DATES

Year	Event
1873	The sport of badminton was brought to England by British soldiers.
1879	First badminton club was organized in New York City (open only to men and beautiful women). Club had 40 original members.
1893	The first national badminton association was formed in England.
1899	Second national badminton organization was formed in Ireland.
1899	First All-England Badminton Championship was held in England. The winner of this tournament has traditionally been called "World Champion."
1903	First international competition: contested between England and Ireland in Dublin.
1907	Badminton Gazette, journal about badminton, was published.
1934	IBF was founded, governing body of international badminton.
1936	ABA was founded, governing body of badminton in the U.S.
1937	First U.S. National Championships were held in Chicago.
1947	First U.S. National Junior Championships were held.
1948	Thomas Cup, international team competition for men, was started.
1956	Uber Cup, international team competition for women, was started.

1966 Devlin Cup, international competition between U.S. and Canada, was started.
1969 First intercollegiate badminton championship for women was started.
1972 Badminton was a trial sport in the Munich Olympic Games.
1975 First intercollegiate badminton championship for men was started.
1975 First professional badminton tournament held in Canada with $19,000 in prizes.
1977 Pan American Games started (open to the Americas; North, Central and South American countries).
1977 WBF was founded, first World Badminton Championships held.
1977 ABA changed organizational structure and name to USBA.
1981 First World Games was founded. (Badminton was included and People's Republic of China made their first appearance in official international competition).

Figure 1

EQUIPMENT

Besides having a facility with a badminton court and net, the special equipment required for playing badminton consists of the racket, shuttlecock and wearing apparel.

Rackets

The badminton racket length, weight or head size is not restricted by the Laws of Badminton. Rackets are generally about 26 inches in length and have wooden handles wrapped with leather grips. Most rackets were wooden until the mid-1950s when steel shaft rackets became popular. Since the mid-1960s and the development of strong and durable light-weight metals, rackets with both metal heads and shafts became popular and now monopolize the market.

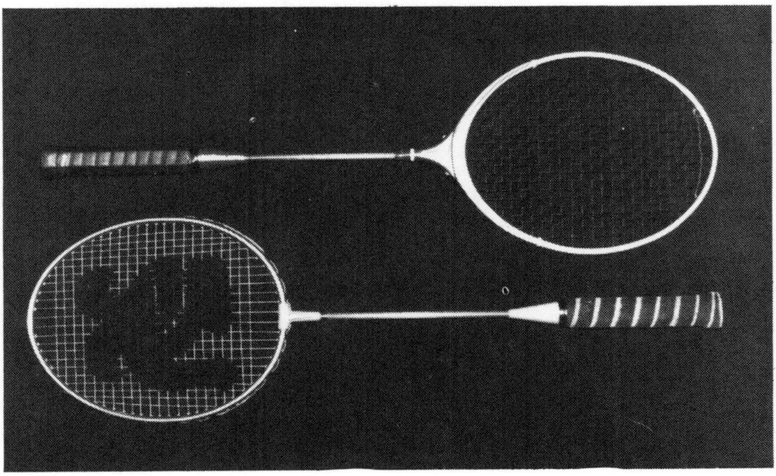

Metal rackets have the advantages over wooden rackets of being more durable and of lighter weight, they can be strung more often and with greater tension, have more flexibility and do not require a press to keep the head from warping. Some players use wooden head rackets because they report the feeling of greater control, however most champions (U.S. and World) use the metal rackets.

In choosing a racket, one should consider the "feel." This is determined by a combination of factors which include weight, balance, flexibility, and grip size.

Strung rackets weigh between 100 and 155 grams (3½-5½ oz.). Competitive players generally prefer light rackets (4 oz. or less).

Racket balance can be determined by measuring the distance from the balance point of the racket to the handle end. Strung rackets balance between 11-13 inches from the handle end. The higher the number, the more head-heavy the racket. Competitive players usually prefer rackets with balance points in the 11-12 inch range so as to increase their speed and maneuverability of the racket.

Racket flexibility is mostly dependent upon the construction material of the racket shaft. The following metals are rated from the most to least flexible respectively: carbon-graphite composition, aluminum, steel.

Grip sizes of 3-3/8, 3½, and 3-5/8 inch circumferences are standard with most racket manufacturers. The smaller grip sizes allow greater maneuverability of the racket in the fingers and more "stroking" control. Hand size should be a major factor in determining grip size.

Most racket manufacturers provide each model of their rackets with a wide variety of weights, balance points, and grip sizes. Competitive players pick out their rackets by "feel." This should be done with strung rackets so the balance point can be determined and air resistance of the strung racket head can be considered when testing the racket.

Stringing

Most rackets are strung with synthetic (nylon) or "gut" strings. Nylon is cheaper, more durable, can be strung tighter, and is less affected by atmospheric conditions. "Gut" gives a little better feel or control because of greater string resilience. The string diameters range from 19-22 gauge (GA) with the highest GA number being the thinnest and least durable string. Rackets are generally strung at tensions between 12-15 lbs. Most competitive players prefer 21-22 GA strings strung at 14-15 lbs.

Excellent tournament rackets are 100-120 grams, 11-12 inch balance point, top grade 21 GA synthetic strings. School grade rackets usually have the following characteristics: 130-140 grams weight, balance — 12½-13 inches, 20 GA strings strung at 12-13 lbs. These specifications are quite satisfactory for learning and playing good badminton. A list of manufacturers can be obtained from the USBA or by consulting the BUSA magazine.

Shuttlecocks

Feather or synthetic shuttlecocks (shuttles) are used for playing badminton. Feather shuttles usually have 16 goose feathers inserted into a kid-covered cork base.

They range in weight between 68 and 80 grams (1/6th oz.), the lighter shuttles being used at high altitudes (i.e., Denver, Mexico City). Most tournament players practice with feather shuttles and all ma-

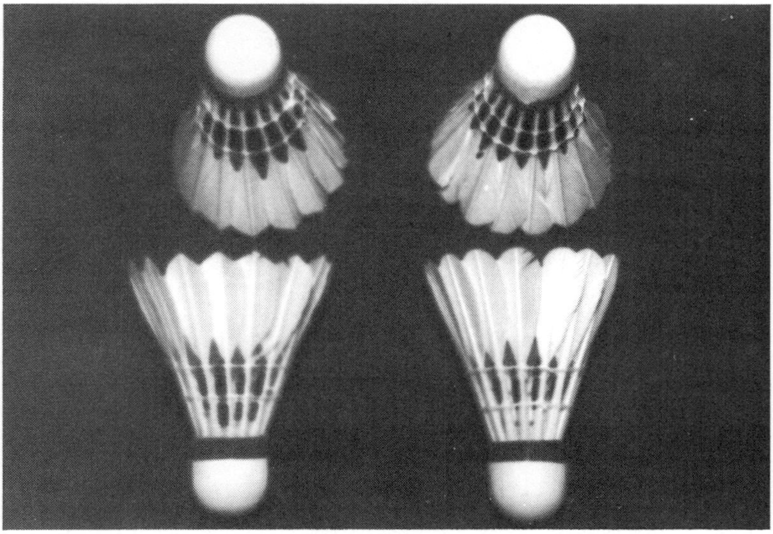

jor tournaments and international competitions use them.

Synthetic shuttles are constructed of plastic or nylon. Most have bases similar to the feather shuttles. These shuttles are usually from 15-25% lighter and tumble end over end more than feather shuttles, thus giving less control and feel, especially during net play. Some come with labels to indicate relative speed. Durability of the synthetic shuttles is at least ten times greater than that of feather shuttles. Some local tournaments, most junior tournaments and schools use synthetic shuttles.

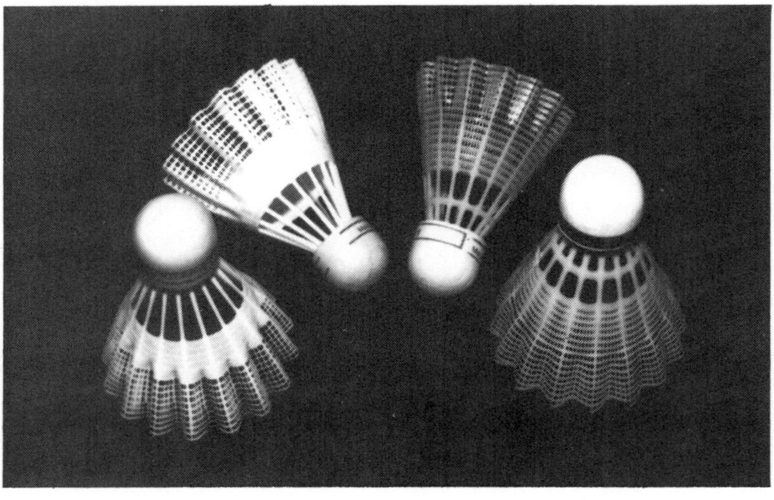

Shuttlecock Care

Proper care of the shuttle can greatly increase its durability and consistency in flight. Primary care depends upon keeping them from getting bent or stepped on during play or storage. Humidification prevents the feathers from becoming brittle and breaking. Tubes of shuttles can be wrapped with a damp towel, stored in a plastic bag or air-tight container containing a moist sponge or towel to humidify the shuttles. Three hours of humidification is generally sufficient. Nylon shuttles should also be humidified as they too tend to get brittle and break if too dry. Plastic shuttles are least resistent to changes in atmospheric conditions, but do not have good flight characteristics or durability as compared to nylon shuttles.

Shuttle Speed

The Laws of Badminton indicate the proper shuttle speed can be tested by hitting a shuttle from the back boundary line with a full underhand stroke parallel to the side line and at an upward angle. If the shuttle is of legal speed, it will land between the opposite long service line for doubles and one foot inside the back boundary line (Figure 2). Some players play with slower shuttles (traveling less distance when tested) which tends to make the game more dependent upon brute strength rather than finesse and tactics.

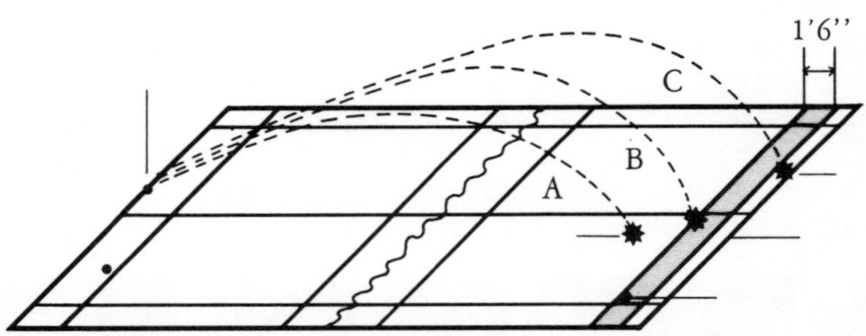

Figure 2: A too slow; B correct speed; C too fast.

The speed of feather shuttles can be altered to conform to the legal speed by tipping (bending the tips of the feathers). The speed will be increased by tipping the feathers inward, and slowed by tipping the feathers outward as shown on page 13.

Players generally begin by tipping every other feather about ¼-inch from the tip of the feather. Speed of feather or synthetic shuttles can be increased by weighting the shuttle by wrapping a ¼-inch circle of athletic tape around the top of the base, or by pushing a thumbtack into the base in the center of the circle where the feathers insert into the base.

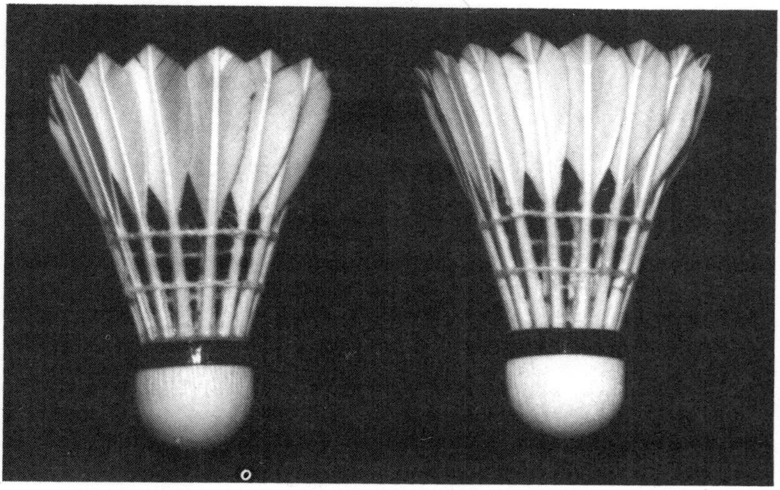

Due to the rising cost and scarcity of goose feathers, synthetic shuttles are increasing in popularity. Recent research and manufacturing developments have improved the flight characteristics of the nylon shuttles and many are approved for tournament competition.

Badminton Clothing

Badminton clothing is similar to that worn for tennis and the other racket sports: shirts and shorts for the men, and tennis dresses or skirts and blouses for the women. The clothing should be comfortable and allow complete freedom for vigorous movement and stretching. Although all-white clothing has been the traditional dress for badminton, only a few clubs and tournament committees still require this standard. Pastel-colored outfits are often worn.

One of the most important clothing items is the badminton (tennis) shoe. In recent years many styles of light, flexible and sturdy shoes, with reinforced toes and good gripping qualities have been developed. These are often sold in pro shops or sporting goods stores. Players should choose shoes that fit comfortably and do not cause blisters or bruises on the toes or heel.

Headbands and wristbands are often worn to help keep perspiration from the eyes and hands, especially in hot and humid climates.

Courts

The Laws of Badminton specify the dimensions of the court and net. The ceiling height should be 30 feet. If less than this, hitting a visible stationary object over the court is ruled a "let" on the serve, and a fault during the other shots of the rally. Hitting a less visible object, i.e., hanging wire, is usually ruled a "let" on all shots.

Floor surfaces have mainly been wooden in America because of the use of indoor school facilities. In recent years, many new surfaces have been developed, some for portable courts, i.e., Tartan, Hova, Boltex, and Supreme surfaces. Players should practice on these surfaces before playing in competition because the sliding and cushioning characteristics may differ drastically from the surface to which they are most accustomed. This precaution may prevent injuries.

GRIPPING, COCKING AND BASIC STROKES

One of the most important aspects of playing badminton is to learn the right way to grip and hold the racket. With proper gripping techniques, one has better opportunity to develop deception, accuracy and power.

Forehand Grip

The racket is considered to be an extension of the arm. When properly held, the face of the racket is parallel to the palm of the racket hand.

In order to find the proper grip on the handle, slide the hand down the shaft, with the palm maintaining a parallel position to the face of the racket. (See photo 1-2 below)

Grip the handle with the ends of the last three fingers placed on the beveled edge of the handle, which is parallel with the face of the racket. (Photo 3 below)

These are considered the gripping fingers. Next, position the index finger in a 'trigger'-like motion around the handle and place the thumb, exerting lateral pressure, directly above the middle finger.

Note that the ball of the thumb rests against the middle finger and not farther up the racket handle. The thumb and index finger are usually considered the source of subtle movements and slight changes of the grip. (Photo 4 top pg. 18)

(1)

(2)

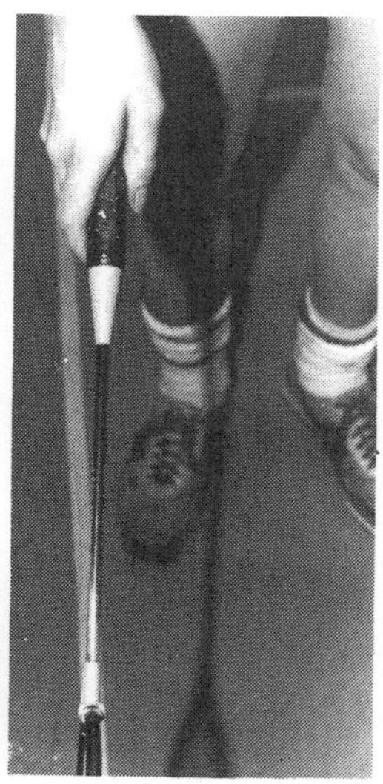

(3)

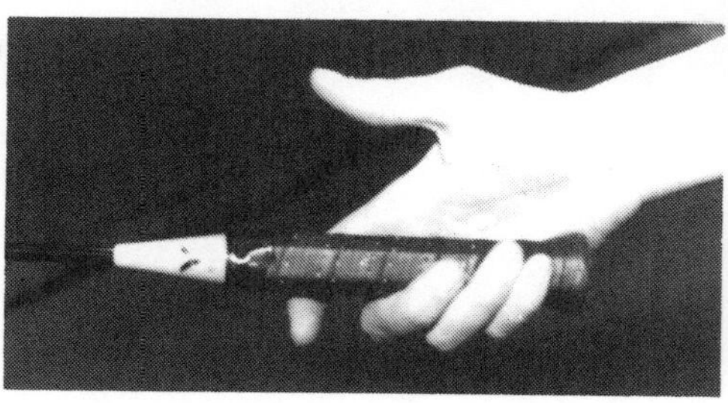

Note that the racket handle is diagonal across the fingers (3).

(4)

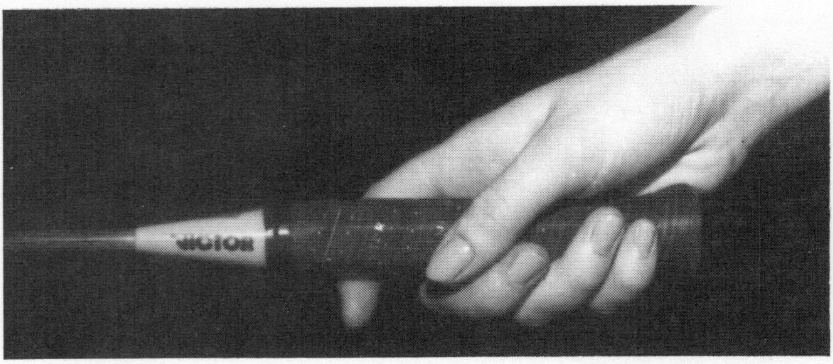

This is the basic grip used for all forehand strokes, however, often position and contact points with the shuttle may dictate slight variations of positions, such as choking up on the handle, as well as different pressure points.

Between shots it is important that the racket is held very loosely to help eliminate muscular tension and to avoid fatigue. One exerts greater pressure with the gripping fingers on the handle during the execution of power strokes as opposed to net play, drop shots, and off-speed shots.

The V-formed junction of the thumb and index finger should be slightly to the left of the top beveled surface of the 8-sided handle.

(5)

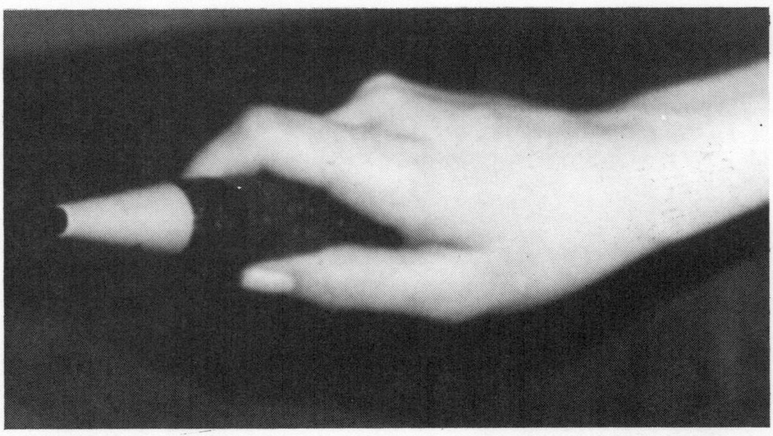

In order to avoid over-gripping the racket, you should be able to slide your left index finger between the V formed by the thumb and the index finger and the top beveled edge of the handle. (Photo 6)

Although the badminton forehand grip is often referred to as the Eastern Forehand tennis grip, the important difference is that the badminton grip emphasizes the handle being held (gripped) with the

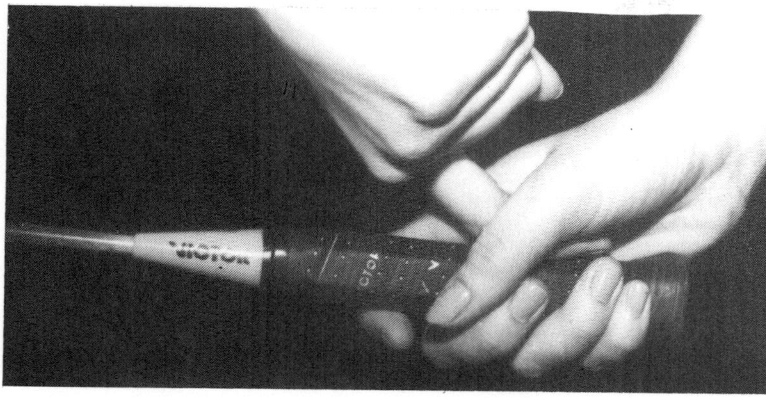

(6)

fingers, whereas in the tennis grip the handle rests more in the palm.

A poor grip is shown below. Note the handle held in palm, no trigger finger, and thumb wrapped too far around racket.

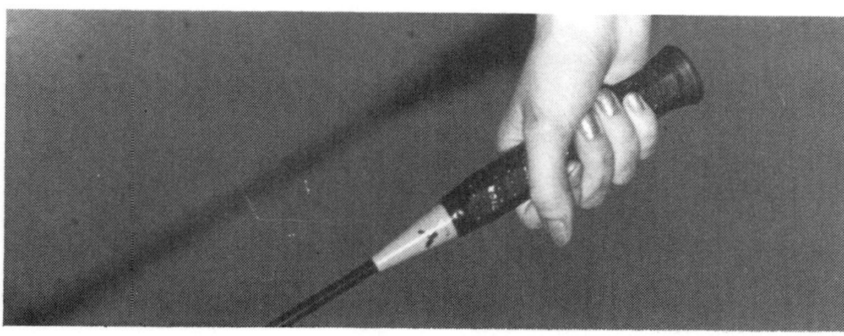

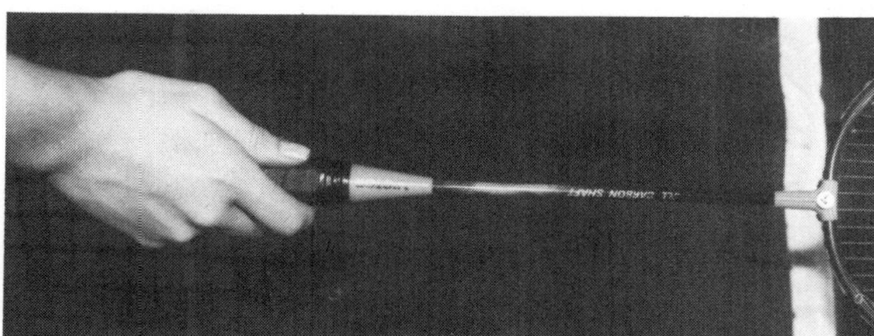

Frying-Pan Grip

Another forehand grip used, particularly for net play, is known as the frying-pan grip. This grip is attained by turning the racket face one-quarter turn in either direction from the normal forehand grip. Note the thumb is lifted to put pressure on the left beveled surface of the handle as shown in the picture above.

Backhand Grip

Although some players may use the basic forehand grip for some backhand shots, there are two basic backhand grips.

The primary backhand grip is similar to the forehand grip with the exception of the thumb placement. Starting from the forehand grip, move the thumb off the middle finger up to the left beveled edge of the handle.

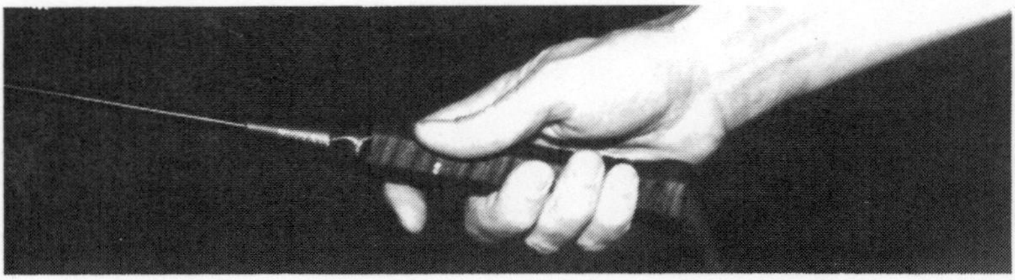

The pressure should be exerted by the inside surface of the thumb on the left beveled edge of the handle. This grip is used for the overhead backhand stroke.

The other backhand grip is often referred to as the "thumbs-up" grip. From the basic forehand grip, the thumbs-up grip is accomplished by rotating the racket one-quarter turn clockwise (right) and moving the thumb up to a position on the top beveled edge of the handle as shown below.

As the thumb moves up, the index finger will move down to a position next to the middle finger.

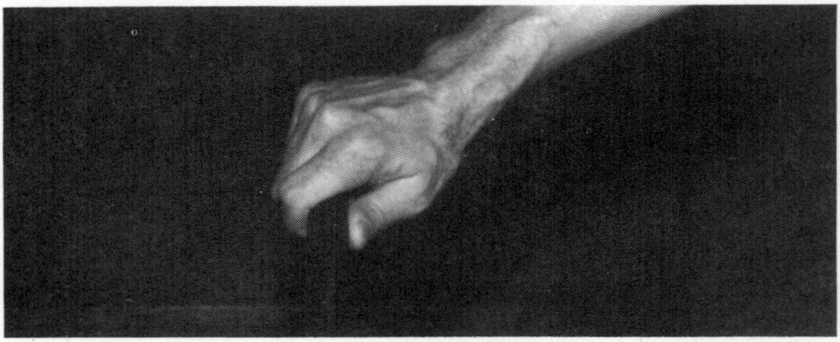

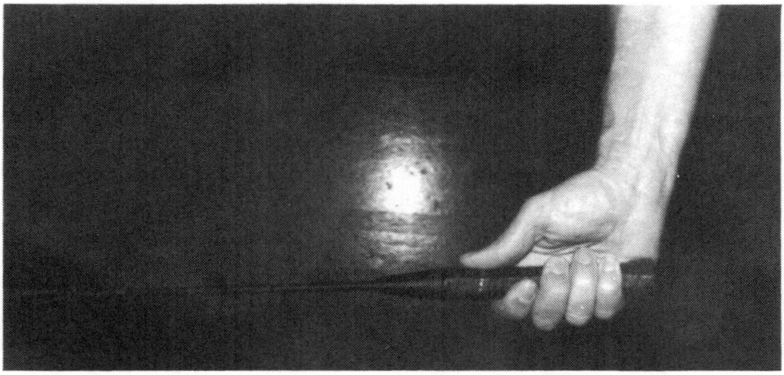

This "thumbs-up" backhand grip is used primarily to block shuttles hit directly at the body, and to execute drives in front of the body. It is not effective for hitting the overhead backhand stroke.

Strokes and shots

In reading the badminton literature the terms "stroke" and "shot" are often used interchangeably. To help clarify and differentiate between the meanings of stroke and shot, the following definitions are applicable. A stroke is a basic hitting pattern, whereas a shot is the resultant speed, angle, and placement of the shuttle.

There are four basic strokes used in the game of badminton: (1) **overhead,** (2) **side-arm,** (3) **underhand,** and (4) **in front of the body** strokes. All of these strokes can be executed from the forehand and the backhand positions, except the in front of the body stroke which is hit with a backhand swinging pattern. Around-the-head shots are executed from the forehand overhead stroking pattern.

There are seven shots which may be used with the various strokes. Shots may vary as to speed, direction and placement on the court. The type of stroke used, as well as the position and placement on the court, dictate the best shots to be executed. The various shots are: (1) **defensive clear,** (2) **attacking clear,** (3) **drive,** (4) **attacking drop,** (5) **loop drop,** (6) **smash,** and (7) **block shot.**

There are three basic phases for each stroking pattern. They are: (1) **preparation phase,** (2) **hitting phase,** and (3) **follow-through phase.**

In the preparation phase, the player moves to the proper court position ready to execute the shot.

The hitting phase consists of a backward motion from the ready position and a forward motion to the point of racket contact with the shuttle.

The follow-through phase is that portion of the swing immediately after contact with the shuttle.

The three basic phases of stroking will be described for each shot hit from the various stroking positions in the following sections of this chapter. However, all of these strokes have the same mechanics of cocking and uncocking. **Learning these mechanics is the most important single aspect of proper stroke development.**

In all forehand strokes the basic cocking position is achieved by hyperextending the wrist and rotating the forearm clockwise (right).

(1)

(2)

Forehand shots are hit from a cocked position to an uncocked position by rotating the forearm counterclockwise (left) and flexing the wrist from the hyperextended to an extended position (photo above right).

Note the wrist should never move to a full-flexed position in uncocking as this movement could cause injury. The wrist should remain extended about 180 degrees from shuttle contact through follow-through[(3) and (S6), Pg. 24]

(3)

(4)

The backhand cocked position is achieved by rotating the forearm and upper arm inward (toward the body), flexing the elbow, and slightly hyperextending the wrist (4). The uncocking is just the opposite, extending the elbow, rotating the forearm and upper arm outward (away from the body), and flexing the wrist to the extended position (see (5) below). The backhand follow-through is completed with wrist hyperextension and complete forearm and upper arm outward rotation (supination (6)).

(5)

(6)

During the cocking phase of the overhead forehand strokes, the right elbow raises and the arm is flexed, the forearm rotates counterclockwise (outward), and the wrist is hyperextended, thus positioning the racket in what is often called the "backscratch" position (below). Teachers often demonstrate this backswing phase of the stroking pattern by touching the racket to the back. However, the actual position of the racket during the backswing rarely comes closer to the body than that shown.

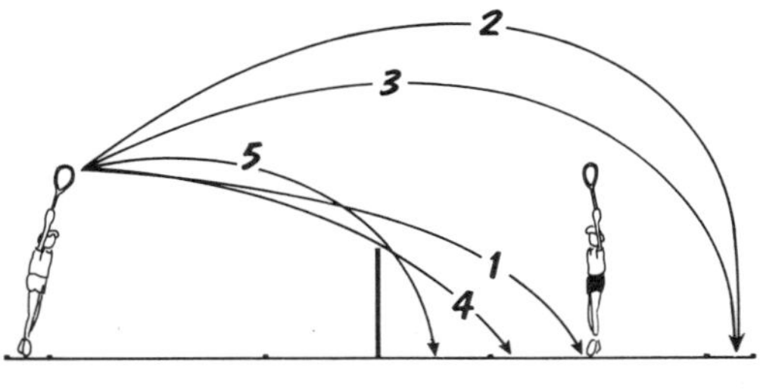

Figure 3

Overhead Strokes (Forehand, Backhand, Around-the-Head)

Shots used for the overhead forehand, backhand, and around-the-head stroke include the following: (1) smash, (2) defensive clear, (3) attacking clear, (4) attacking drop, and (5) loop drop. (Figure 3).

Smash Shot

The smash is considered the ultimate attacking shot. It is usually employed as the put-away shot or the point-getter. The basic mechanics of the smash are shown in Photographs S1-S-7.

The smash is executed the same as the other overhead power strokes (clears), however it is hit with greater velocity and the racket angle is such to give a trajectory in a downward plane (Figure 4c). Basically, the smash is an extension of the attacking and defensive clear shots in that all shots from the overhead stroke should look the same upon contact with the shuttle.

(S1-7)

Defensive Clear Shot

The primary purpose of the defensive clear shot is to hit the shuttle high and deep near the back boundary line to allow the player time to get back to the center of the court in good receiving position. This shot is not considered a point-getter, but may be used effectively to fatigue your opponent.

The basic mechanics to execute the defensive clear shot from the overhead stroke is similar to that of the smash, but the racket head is at such an angle at contact to give the shuttle a high trajectory. (Figure 3, 4a).

Attacking Clear Shot

The primary purpose of the attacking clear shot is to get the shuttle behind your opponent. It is used either as a point-getter or to set up for the next shot. Like the defensive clear shot, the basic mechanics are the same as for the smash except upon contact with the shuttle. The racket head is more perpendicular to the net, thus giving a relatively flatter trajectory (Figure 3, 4b). The trajectory should be high enough to clear your opponent's racket and have the shuttle land near the back boundary line of the court.

Attacking Drop Shot

The attacking drop shot is similar to the smash and is sometimes referred to as a controlled smash in that it is hit with less velocity than

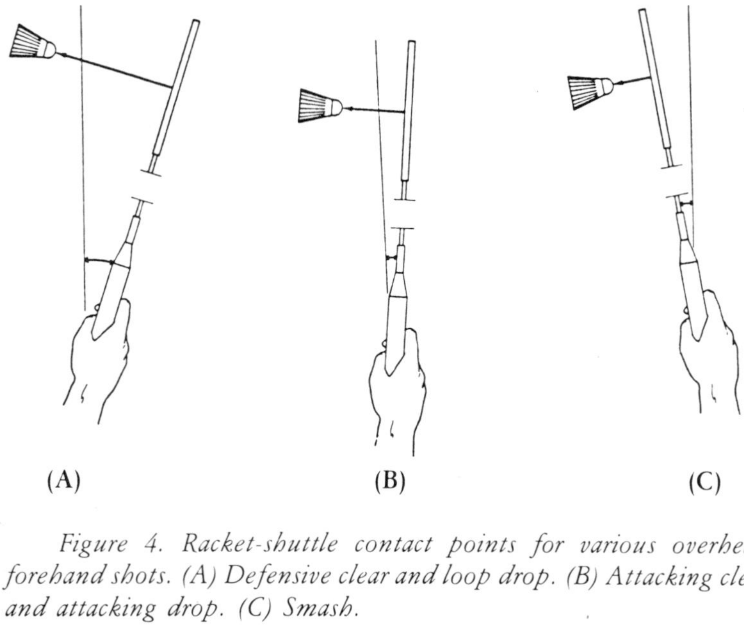

(A) (B) (C)

Figure 4. Racket-shuttle contact points for various overhead forehand shots. (A) Defensive clear and loop drop. (B) Attacking clear and attacking drop. (C) Smash.

the smash. It is considered a point-getter if your opponent is out of position, or as a quick shot used to make your opponent lift the shuttle, thus giving you the attack.

The basic mechanics for the attacking drop shot are the same as the other overhead strokes except that the racket head, upon shuttle contact, is angled to project a downward flight.(Figure 3, 4b).

Loop Drop Shot

The primary purpose of the loop drop shot is to bring your opponent in, close to the net, to set a pattern of running from net to backcourt and back to net again. This shot is generally not a point-getter, but is used to run your opponent longer distances. The basic mechanics are the same as the other overhead strokes except that the racket head, upon shuttle contact, is similar to that of the defensive clear. (Figure 3, 4a). Note lack of follow-through (D1-2) and S7, Pg. 24.

Both attacking and loop drop shots are hit with less force than the power shots (clears and smashes). In order to create deception, the follow-through of the drop shots can take one of three patterns: slice, straight ahead, and reverse cut. (See below D4, D5, D3, respectively).

(D 1-5)

Around-the-Head Stroke

The around-the-head stroke is used to hit shuttles on the left side of the body which can be hit with a forehand overhead pattern utilizing an arc around the head and above the left shoulder. With this stroke you can achieve the power of a forehand stroke to hit shots on the backhand side of the body. This stroke provides the opportunity to execute all of the basic shots from the overhead forehand stroke, which are smashes, defensive and attacking clears, and loop and attacking drops. The around-the-head stroke has the advantage of being deceptive as well as powerful. This stroke allows a player to cover approximately three-quarters of the backcourt with the forehand stroking pattern, leaving about one-quarter for the backhand strokes. This stroke should not be used to hit the shuttle in the backhand area of the court, since it takes you too far from the center of the court, leaving you in poor position to retrieve the next shot.

The basic mechanics of the around-the-head stroke are similar to the forehand overhead stroke except the body is angled toward the left side of the court, and body momentum is carried away from the center of the court. Thus, this stroke is characterized by footwork in which the player hits off the right foot with the body rotating to the left and landing deeper in the court on the left foot.

AHS 1. Around-the-head stroke. Take-off on right foot.
AHS 2. Around-the head stroke. Just prior to recovery on left leg.

Backhand Overhead Stokes

The following shots may be hit from the backhand overhead stroke: (1) smash, (2) defensive clear, (3) attacking clear, (4) attacking drop, and (5) loop drop.

The basic mechanics of the overhead backhand stroke are relatively simple, but often seem very difficult for the learner. The following techniques will provide the player with a strong repertoire of backhand overhead shots.

1. It is preferable to use the primary backhand grip when learning the backhand overhead stroking pattern. The "thumbs-up" backhand grip should not be used for overhead strokes from a position deep in the court. (Pg. 20 top photo)
2. From the ready position, the player will turn 180 degrees and prepare to hit backhand overhead shots stepping onto the right foot with his back facing the net.
3. The overhead backhand swinging pattern will start with a backswing from the ready position (elbow down and racket head up). During the backswing, the player will flex his arm, point the elbow toward the anticipated point of racket-shuttle contact, rotate the forearm inward and hyperextend the wrist. (BO 1-2)

4. The forward swing begins with pointing the upper arm toward the sideline, extending the arm at the elbow, rotating the forearm outward, and flexing the wrist from the hyperextended position. This swing is similar to a judo chop motion during which the hand moves from a thumbs-down to a thumbs-up position at racket-shuttle contact. (BO 3-4)

5. The backhand overhead stroke is hit on a plane with the upper arm extended at an angle between the horizontal and a 30 degree elevation. Thus the shuttle is hit with the arm extended to the side and only slightly above head height, but not over the head or right shoulder. (BO 4, BO 6)

It is essential that the upper arm be directed toward the sideline and not follow through toward the net. (BO 5)

6. The follow-through of the backhand overhead stroke consists primarily of hyperextension of the wrist. This allows the racket to follow through with the racket head pointing toward the net for the power shots. (BO 5)
7. The follow-through for the backhand overhead drop is very short, with the racket head pointed upward. (BO 7-8)
8. Efficient backhand overhead stroking depends on a rhythmic swing with rapid acceleration of the racket head, using the "judo chop" motion. The player should concentrate on timing rather than power. The shuttle should be hit at the players' side and not at a point between the player and the net.

BO1-8

With the basic mechanics described above, it is possible to hit clears, drops, and smashes with a deceptive stroking pattern. As stroking skills develop, the backhand shots are generally more deceptive, but less powerful, than the forehand shots. Similar to the forehand overhead stroke, the racket head angle and velocity of the swing will determine whether a smash, defensive clear, attacking clear, attacking drop or loop drop is being hit.

Side-Arm Stroke (Forehand, Backhand)

Shots hit from the forehand and backhand side-arm stroking pattern include the following: (1) drives, (2) drop, (3) defensive clear, and (4) attacking clear. (Figure 5).

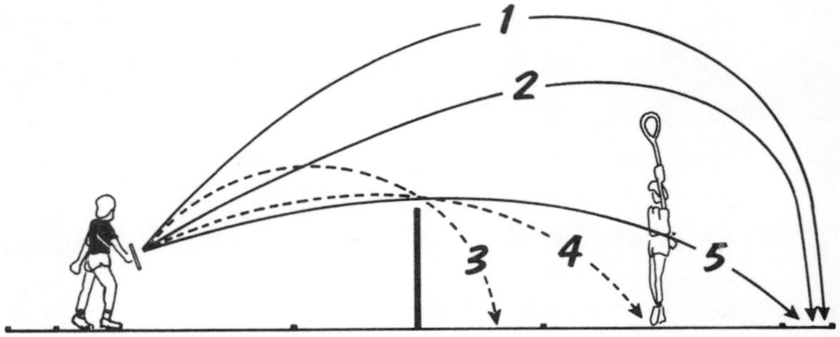

Figure 5. Sidearm stroke shuttle flight pattern. (1) Defensive Clear. (2) Attacking Clear. (3) Loop Drop. (4) Half Court Drive. (5) Hard Drive.

Drive Shots (Cross-Court, Straight Ahead)

In executing the drive shot, the shuttle is hit close to net height, carrying either deep in the court or half-court, depending upon the force applied to the shot. The drive shot is used primarily in doubles and mixed doubles play.

FS1-8

The basic mechanics in the forehand side-arm stroke is leading with the elbow and pronating the arm at the extension of the stroke. (Photos FS 1-6). For the backhand side-arm stroke, lead with the elbow, straighten the arm and rotate the arm outward. (Photos BS 1-4).

BS1-6

Drop Shots (Cross-Court, Straight Ahead)

Like the drive shot, the drop shot is executed with the same mechanics, except the velocity of the uncocking is reduced at shuttle-racket contact for both forehand (Photos FS 7-8) and backhand straight ahead at cross-court (Photos BS 5-6) side-arm drops and the racket does not follow through toward the net.

Defensive Clear Shot (Forehand, Backhand)

In executing the defensive clear shot from the side-arm stroke, the basic mechanics are the same for the side-arm drive. Upon contact, however, the racket is angled to hit the shuttle high and deep in the court. (Figure 5).

Attacking Clear Shot

The basic mechanics of hitting attacking clear shots from the side-arm stroking pattern are similar to that of the drive, but the trajectory is angled lower than the defensive clear and higher than the drive. (Figure 5).

Note the racket head should be kept above hand level in executing the side-arm stroke. (Photos FS 7, FS 8, BS 3, page 31).

In summary, when using either the forehand or backhand side-arm stroke, the following four basic shots are: (1) drive, (2) drop, (3) defensive clear, and (4) attacking clear.

Underhand Stroke (Forehand, Backhand)

The underhand stroke is used primarily when the shuttle is lower than the height of the net tape and, usually, between the short service line and the net. The two basic shots executed when using the underhand stroke are the defensive clear and the drop.

The use of the underhand is also required in the serve and will be discussed in that section.

Defensive Clear Shot

The purpose of this shot is to clear the shuttle high and deep near the back boundary line, thus allowing the player time to get back to the center of the court for good defense. The shot is also effective in making your opponent move to the deepest position in the court in order to tire him out.

The basic mechanics of the forehand underhand stroke, when making a defensive clear shot, are to have a cocked position and uncock by rotating the arm in a counterclockwise motion. (Photos FUC 1-4). For the backhand, go to the shuttle in a cocked position and rotate the arm in a clockwise motion. (Photos BUC 1-4, page 34).

Note shuttle is hit well in front of the body. *FUC 1-4*

BUC 1-4

Drop Shot

In this shot the shuttle should be contacted as high above the floor as possible. The purpose of the shot is to bring your opponent close to the net.

The basic mechanics are to make contact with the shuttle in a cocked positon and use the arm to lift the shuttle over the net in a "hairpin" trajectory. (Photos FUD 1-3). If contact with the shuttle is made low on the net, a cross-court drop shot should be made. (FUD 4-6) The mechanics of the backhand underhand drop are shown in Photos BUD 1-6.

FUD 1-6

BUD 1-3 straight drop. BUD 4-6 cross-court drops. BUD 1-6

Underhand Shots

When moving toward the net to hit an underhand shot, the player must decide early on whether the shot will be a defensive clear or drop shot. The defensive clear has a longer backswing preparation, whereas the backswing for the drop is accomplished in front of the body (see side view of forehand and backhand defensive clear and drop preparations — FUC 1, BUC 1, FUD 1, BUD 1, pages 33-35).

If the player decides to hit a drop return, the final foot placement will prepare for the straight-ahead or cross-court return. The leg will lunge directly toward the contact point for the straight-ahead return, whereas for the cross-court return, the last step will be closer to the sideline so the swing will carry the shot back across the body for the cross-court shot. (FUD 6, BUD 6)

The cross-court shot should not be played from the center court net position as these shots often carry outside the width of the court due to a harder hit than the straight-ahead drop.

The underhand shot can be very deceptive because a drive or attacking clear can be hit from the same preparation as the drop if the shuttle is contacted high enough and far enough back from the net.

In summary, when using the underhand stroke, whether forehand or backhand, there are two basic shots: (1) defensive clear, and (2) drop shot (straight ahead, cross-court).

In Front of the Body Stroke (Backhand)

This stroke is used to return a shot smashed or driven at the body. The basic returns are: (1) block drop, (2) drives, and (3) clears.

Block Drop

The purpose of this shot is basically a defensive return of a smash by your opponent. Sometimes this shot is a point-getter in that it is a quick return and, if placed in the right spot, will result in an offensive shot.

The basic mechanics are to extend the arm out to meet the shuttle in a cocked position using the "thumbs-up" backhand grip. (Photos FBS 1-5). It is important that the elbow be in front of the body to provide room for the backswing. (FBS 1-3)

Defensive Clear Shot

The purpose of this shot is to give yourself time to get back to the center of the court.

The basic mechanics of this shot are the same as the block shot except, when hitting the shuttle, uncock and rotate the arm in a counterclockwise motion.

FBS 1-5

Drive

This shot is usually used to reverse the attack and direct the shuttle quickly past the front court player in the attacking doubles formation.

The basic mechanics of the in front of the body drive shot are the same as the defensive clear except the trajectory is low and flat. The velocity can be that of a half-court drive or a deep drive. (FBS 4-5)

In summary, when using the in front of the body stroke, there are three basic shots: (1) block shot, (2) defensive clear, and (3) drive shot.

High, Deep Serve

This serve is an underhand forehand serve hit high so that the shuttle will land in deep court, near the back line. Photos HS 1-12.

Basic Techniques

A. Starting position — hit from a stationary position. Both feet must remain in contact with the court since "stepping in" is a fault.

B. Straighten arm — wrist cocked.
C. Rotate body.
D. Shift weight — right to left foot.
E. Uncock wrist — upon contact with the bird.
F. Bird contact point for legal serve — bottom of server's hand must not be below top of racket head.
G. Follow-through — bird contact is made well in front of the body, not at the side, on a follow-through of an underhand stroke in a vertical plane.

Low, Short Serve

This serve should be made on a flat trajectory so that it will barely clear the net and hit close to the short line in the opponent's court.

Basic Techniques

All basic techniques for the low, short serve — starting position, rotate body, etc., are the same as for the deep, high serve except:

A. This is a "push" type serve, accomplished by wrist remaining almost fully cocked throughout the serve, with little rotation of the forearm. Photos FSS 1-6.
B. Attempt to contact the bird as close to waist height as possible to achieve the desired flat trajectory.

Drive Serve

The drive serve is comparable to hitting a line drive in baseball. This serve can be driven at the opponent preferably to hit just below the shoulder level. (Photos FDS 1-4)

Basic Techniques

All basic techniques — starting position, rotate body, etc., for the drive serve are the same as for the deep, high serve except:

A. The racket is partially uncocked at contact with the bird.

B. Since the racket does not go beyond half cock, there is not a complete follow-through in a full arc, as in the high, deep serve.

Flick Serve

This serve is one of a player's better deception shots. It should be used primarily if your opponent is rushing the net on low, short serves. It is used mainly in doubles and mixed doubles play. (FFS 1-2, Pg. 40.)

Basic Techniques

The same basic techniques apply as to starting position, arm, body rotation, etc., except:

A. This serve has every appearance of being a low, short serve, since the forearm is fully cocked approaching the bird.

B. At the instant before contact, the forearm should be rotated to flick the bird over the opponents' heads.

Backhand Service (Right-Handed Player) Photos Pg. 42

A. Stand within inches of the intersection of the center and short service lines (at the T) and face the center of the receiver's court.

B. Hold the shuttle by the tip of one feather between the thumb and index finger of the left hand. The left elbow should touch the body about six inches lateral to the midline. The left arm should be in such position that the shuttle is about three inches to the left of the midline, about 6-8 inches below the waist and about 9-10 inches in front of the body.

C. The racket is held with a backhand grip, the right thumb being placed against the side of the handle which is parallel to the plane of the racket head.

D. The racket head is placed against the server's clothing in such position that the middle point of the strings is about 6-8 inches below the waist and about three inches to the left of the midline.

E. From the above basic service position, the server views the net or his opponent rather than the shuttle during delivery of the service.

F. For the short service, the shuttle is hit primarily by extending the forearm in a short, quick motion. The wrist is broken (flexed laterally) only for drive and flick serves to gain the needed power.

G. This service is best practiced by hitting against a wall until a rhythm is established that feels comfortable and the service procedures are standardized.

In brief, the low, short service can be hit very accurately and should be the primary service in doubles events. Consistent service can be achieved best by standardizing the backhand service procedures. Drive and flick serves should be used sparingly to provide variety and a change of pace.

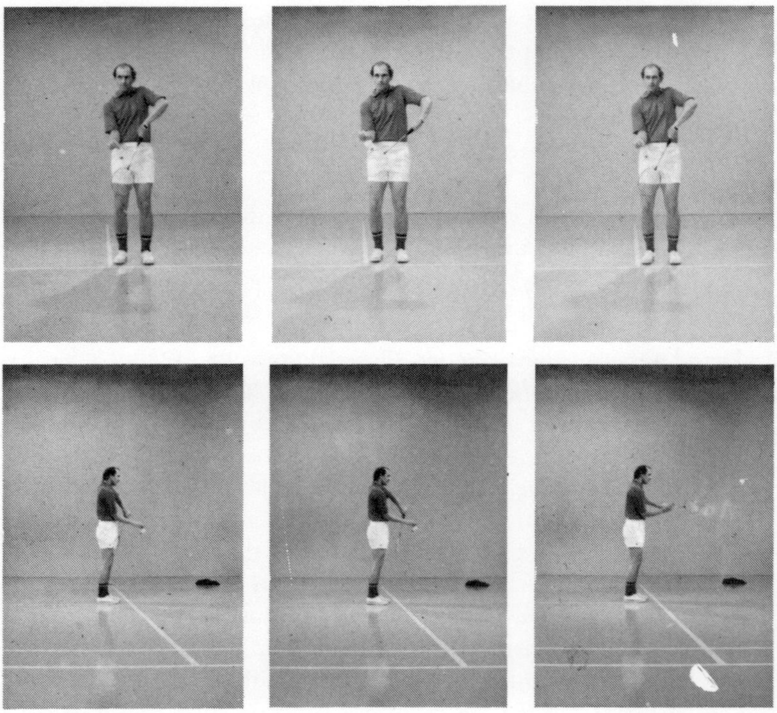

Upside-Down Backhand Service

In the early 1980s, Malaysian players developed a backhand doubles service in which the shuttle was struck with a slicing motion across the feathers while the shuttle was held by the base with the feathers pointed downward. Striking of the feathers caused the shuttle to take an unpredictable flight pattern and often appear to 'dive' downward and laterally after passing over the net. In 1982 the International Badminton Federation ruled this service to be illegal. Service rules require the shuttle to be dropped from the hand and be struck on the cork position rather than the feathers. The basic backhand service as outlined above is legal.

Movement Techniques

Once the proper stroking techniques have been mastered, errors will generally result from not being in proper position to execute the desired shot. The more quickly and efficiently the player can move about the court, the better position he will be in to attack the shuttle with a variety of deceptive shots, or return the attacking shots of the opponent.

The rest of this chapter will consider the following techniques of badminton movement patterns:

1. The ready position.
2. Center of gravity and speed-line concepts of movement.
3. How to get started, which foot moves first, where and why.
4. The final step before striking the shuttle.
5. Techniques for returning to the base and ready position.

Ready Position

Badminton is a very dynamic game in which the time available to move from the base position to contacting the shuttle is about .95 seconds for singles, and about .85 seconds for doubles. Considering these very short lapses of time between shots, it becomes obvious that the ready position is only a "dynamic position." This ready position is assumed during the time period the retriever is orienting himself to

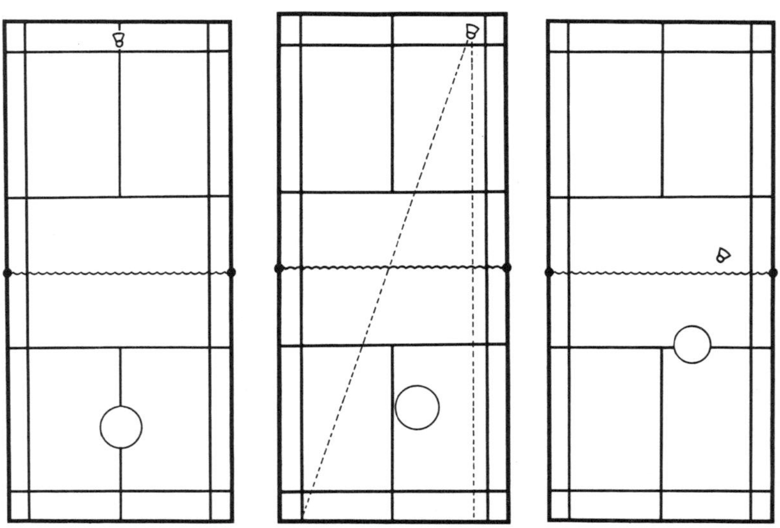

Figure 6 *A* *B* *C*

where the shuttle is being hit, and making the initial preparations to move toward the shuttle. Thus, the ready position might be more accurately described as a movement pattern than as a position.

Ideally, this position is taken near the center of the player's court and is called the "base position." The base position varies depending upon the point from which your opponent is hitting the shuttle. Figure 6A depicts the position a receiver takes when the shuttle is being hit from the deep center area of the court. Figure 6B depicts a more lateral position when the shuttle is being hit from the deep sideline, and Figure 6C depicts the forward and lateral base position occurring when the shuttle is hit from a low position very close to the net. Thus, the base position reflects from where the shuttle is being hit and the anticipated variety of shots that can be made. As can be seen in Figure 6B, the base position is equidistant from power shots (dotted lines) that can be hit to the back court side positions.

When a player expects a smash, or his opponent is in position to execute any shot (clear, drop, smash), as during a high, deep singles service return, the ready position should have the feet approximately parallel to the net (perpendicular to the direct line from the shuttle to the defensive player) as shown in Figure 7. This position allows for the quickest movement toward either sideline.

During a rally in which a player is moving from either the net or backcourt toward the base position and the anticipated opponent's return is a drop or clear, a ready position with one foot in front of the other and almost perpendicular to the net should be taken (Figure 8).

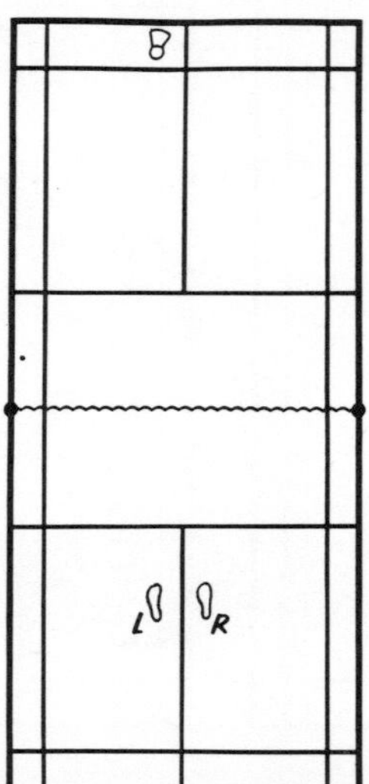

Figure 7

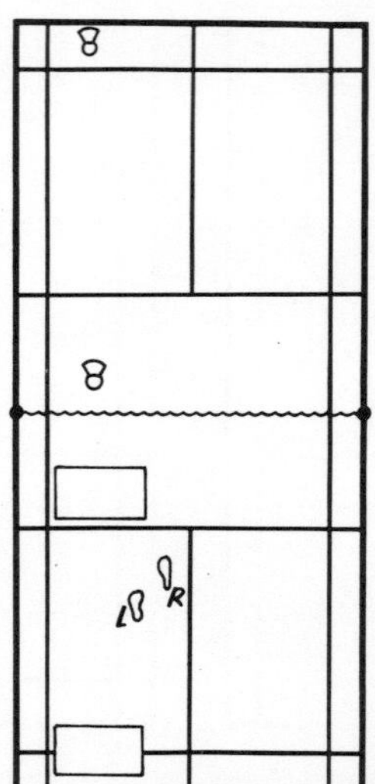

Figure 8

Efficient movement patterns do not favor the use of dominant or non-dominant foot for initial or final steps, but rather, this is determined by the position of the player on the court and from where the opponent is hitting the shuttle. If a player anticipates a drop to the front right of the court or a clear to the deep left of the court, his feet should be set up on a speed-line on this diagonal with his right foot forward (Figure 9-A). However, if he expects to be moving on a diagonal from the left forecourt to the right backcourt, a speed-line should be established with the left foot forward (Figure 9-B). Thus, it makes no difference whether the player is left- or right-handed, or left- or right-footed.

Arm and Racket Position

In most situations, the racket arm should be flexed to about 90 degrees, with the racket held in front of the body. The racket head will be approximately shoulder height. The grip should be the basic forehand grip. (Photo FBS 1, Pg. 37)

In doubles, or in situations of very quick exchanges, a backhand grip may be most effective. This depends on one's ability to anticipate the expected shot.

Body Position

Regardless of the foot placement, the body must make a rhythmical move or slight bounce as the shuttle is being struck by the opponent. The center of gravity will drop slightly by flexion of the knees, hip and spinal column. In order to avoid a false start, the feet will be spread at least shoulder-width to enable one to maintain stability while the

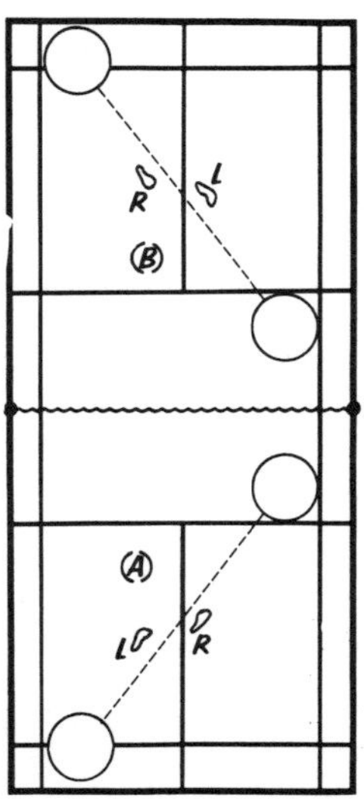

Figure 9

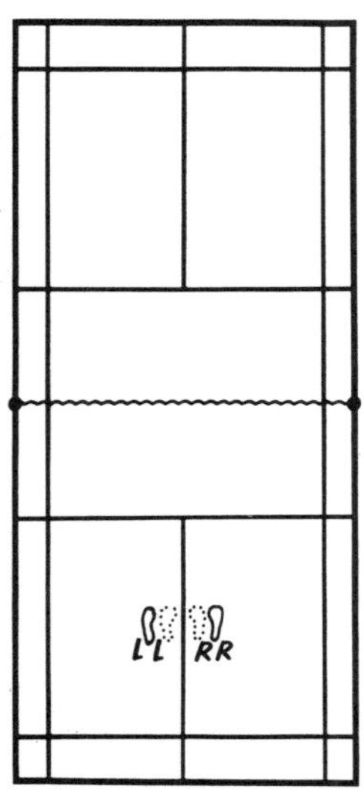

Figure 10

opponent is hitting with a deceptive motion. The better the opponent's deceptiveness in stroking or the more options for the return, the more important it is that a lower and wider stance be taken in assuming the ready position (Figure 10). In addition, a lower and wider stance will also be assumed by the faster and more powerful player in moving back to the base position, thus enabling the player to stop and maintain stability. (See Figure 10).

Basic Footwork

The ability to get a quick start is essential to playing badminton. Unfortunately, few people realize that there are some very specific and essential techniques which are best employed to accomplish this movement pattern efficiently. Although it seems obvious that one must assume a running position and move in the direction of the shuttle, two basic movements which are not so obvious must be accomplished to achieve this requirement. These movements will be described starting from the basic ready position with the feet parallel to the net (Figure 10). The feet will be spread at least shoulder width and foot plant (remember, this is a dynamic position or movement) will occur about the time of shuttle contact by the opponent. All movement patterns will follow the center of gravity method of movement, and the establishment of the anticipated "speed-line." These two methods establish the feet in a potential running position in a direction of movement to the final body position at racket contact with the shuttle.

Movement to the Front Right Corner of the Court

The first movement should be with the left foot slightly back and

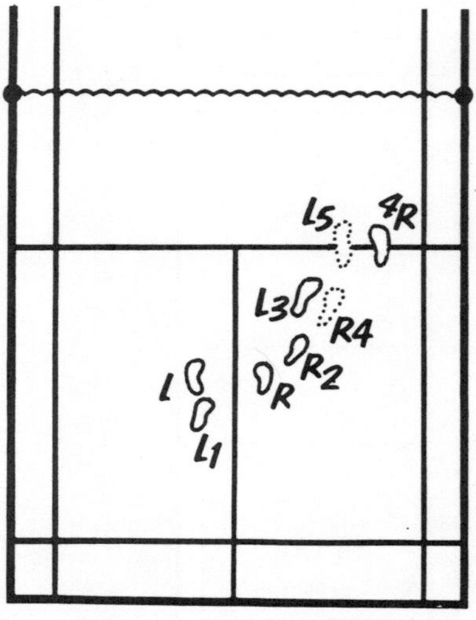

Figure 11

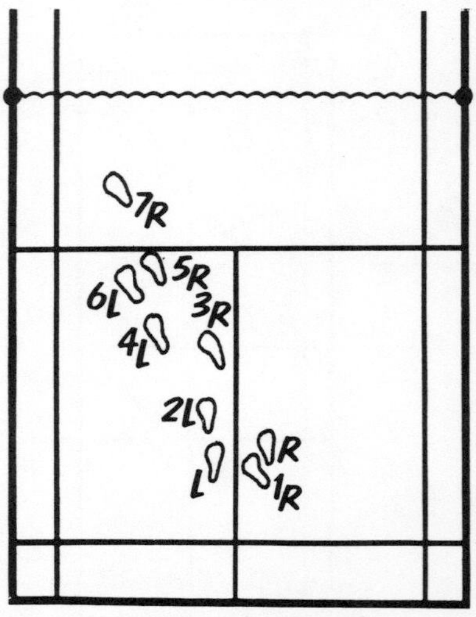

Figure 12

with a pivot so the foot is lined up pointing in the direction of the desired movement (Figure 11). The first two steps are very rapid and establish the direction of movement. As soon as the right foot is raised off the floor, the body is able to move very quickly due to the influence of the center of gravity being farther in front of the left foot than if there was not the quick first step slightly backwards (Figure 11). The first two steps provide a great deal of acceleration which is continued during the third step. Figure 12 shows the movement pattern to the left, and illustrates a case where the player was unable to get back to the center of his court. Hence, he establishes a base a little deeper in the court than in Figure 11. Note the movement pattern to the left begins on the right foot and is a mirror image of the movement to the right. Since this movement pattern was farther (Figure 12), and knowing that the last step must be taken with the right foot, a short shuffle or 'chasse' step (step 6) in which the left leg takes a shortened step so the final step can be a full lunge to the shuttle with the right leg (step 7) is made. Depending on how far the player must move to hit the shuttle, the chasse step will be used to ensure the final step is taken with the racket leg.

Forward Movement

A. The final step should be made with the racket foot (right foot for right-handed player, and left foot for left-handed player).

B. The final step should be long and with body erect from waist upward. (See Photo 48). This type of movement pattern is common in fencing. This final step should be a powerful movement (forceful). (Photos Pg. 33-35)

C. The final step should be taken which allows shuttle contact to be made so the racket will intercept shuttle in front of the body. (Photos Pg. 33-35)

D. The racket-arm elbow should be almost directly over racket-leg knee as the shuttle is being hit.

E. Racket stroke (for right-handed player). (Photos Pg. 33-34)

   1. The racket should be slightly in front of body during the final lunge step.
   2. The wrist, cocked back with shoulder flexion and elbow extended, will give the greatest range of motion, and allow the shuttle to be deceptively hit at the last moment.
   3. This pattern of movement (stroking) will allow for an easy drop shot by contacting the shuttle with a cocked wrist near the net.
   4. This movement pattern will allow clears, drives and flicks off the net with a deceptive stroke by uncocking the wrist at the time of contact of racket and shuttle

The above movement pattern is crucial and must be very smooth and rhythmical. Rather than having to make stroking adjustments by reaching with the arm for the shuttle, the final footwork lunge should place the body in a position to allow for a comfortable, smooth stroking pattern which is quite similar for every return.

Movement to both the forehand and backhand side of the court should be similar with the final step being made with the racket foot.

Movement to shuttles which are hit in front of the body should be played with the backhand strokes.

The key error one should try to avoid in stroking after movement toward the net is to move the racket head in front of the body and then bring the racket back in order to swing forward again at the shuttle. This pattern is not rhythmical or efficient and often prevents the player from hitting a drop shot.

The non-racket hand will usually extend about 180 degrees in opposition to the racket hand to keep balance during most strokes with the lunging movement to the net. (Photo Pg. 34 BUC 1-4). The last step is generally long and powerful, and the body should be as erect as possible from the waist up.

For movement patterns which require a very long lunge or last step for the player to reach the shuttle, the non-racket leg should be brought up nearly to the other foot to allow for rhythmical execution of the stroke and follow-through, and to move the player into a position to return efficiently toward the center of the court by the center of gravity method of movement (Figure 13, 5th step, shuttle is hit on the 4th step). This movement pattern also has the advantage of equalizing the forces exerted by each leg as opposed to having the racket leg do all

the work in stopping the movement after the lunge, and then push the body back toward the base.

Backward Movement Patterns

Movement to the forehand baseline follows the same principles that apply to movement toward the net. As can be seen in Figure 14A, the first step in moving to the deep forehand court is taken with the left foot in a short move toward the net, and a slight counterclockwise pivot. Almost simultaneously, the right foot moves toward the baseline. The right foot placement will establish the speed-line between the left foot and anticipated movement to where the shuttle is hit (Figure 14A). The player will continue backward movement with steps 3 and 4 (and 5 and 6) depending on how deep in the court he must move to reach the shuttle. The player will stroke the shuttle while moving off the right foot (step 4 or 6) and rotating the body counterclockwise. The left foot (step 5 or 7) will then catch the body which is leaning back toward the net and the right foot will take the first step back toward the base position (Figure 14B). The above footwork pattern is used in controlled situations, returning defensive clears or services.

Under pressure situations, retrieving an attacking clear, the player will pivot clockwise during the short step toward the net and plant the right foot completing the turn. Thus, the player is running with his back toward the net (Figure 15). The player will make a powerful jump and lunge off the left leg (step 3) and hit the shuttle from an airborne position (body rotation counterclockwise) with the right leg catching the body. The dotted lines in Figure 15 show the recovery and movement back toward the base on steps 5 and 6. All power shots and drops should be included in the player's selection of shots from both of the above movement patterns to the baseline.

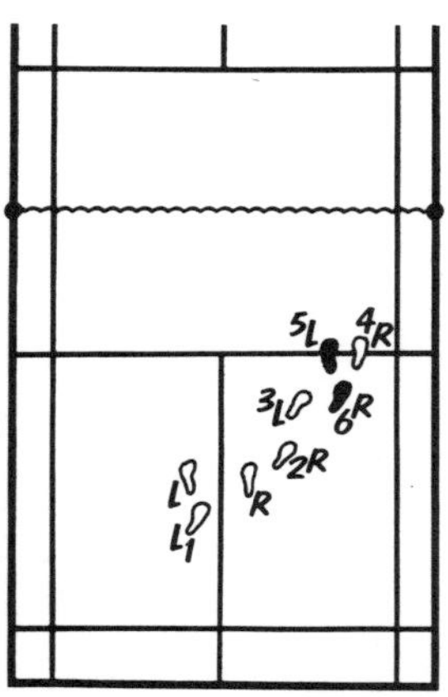

Figure 13

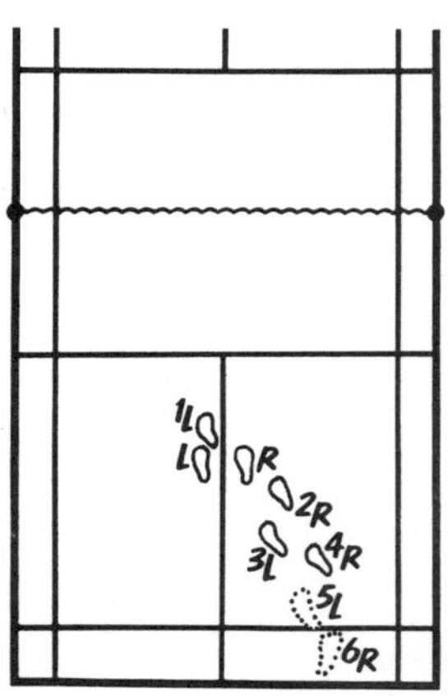

Figure 14A

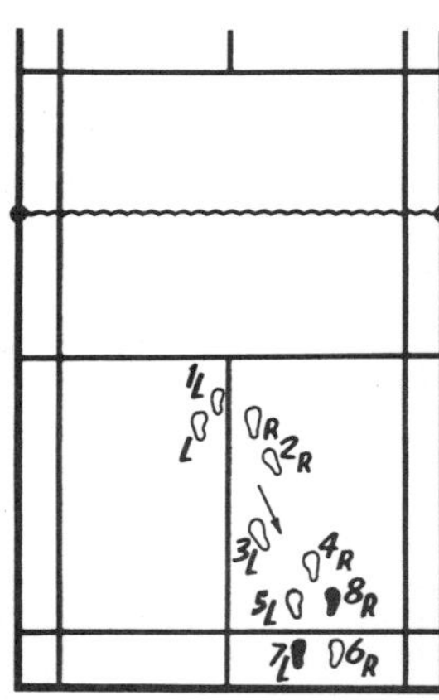

Figure 14B

Many people erroneously think that there should be foot contact with the floor for power shots, however, one of the major contributions to the force of the shot is the rotation of the body counterclockwise about 90°. The body rotates better when the feet are not in contact with the floor. Thus, there will be a powerful push with the foot, body rotation, and hitting of the shuttle while the body is in the air. Proficient players hit almost all shots from the baseline with this technique, as do tennis players hitting the serve.

Backhand

Movement to the backhand baseline is very similar to the mirror image of the pattern to the forehand (Figure 15) except that the speedline will be set up to move in a line that is directed no farther than about three feet from the sideline (Figure 16). On the backhand, it is desirable not to be cramped in the stroking, thus there is no need to move any farther toward the sideline than about three feet from it. A decision must be made as to whether the shot will be hit from a backhand or an around-the-head stroke at the beginning of the movement pattern. This is important because many people start to move for the around-the-head stroke and discover that they are late, and try to play a backhand. They move too close to the sideline and cramp the stroke. On the forehand side it is good technique to stay close to the shuttle because it is desirable to make contact with the shuttle overhead, and the body will not be cramped.

Racket contact with the shuttle and the final foot placement (Step 5 in Figure 16) will occur almost simultaneously and often the foot plant occurs slightly after the hit. (Photo Pg. 48)

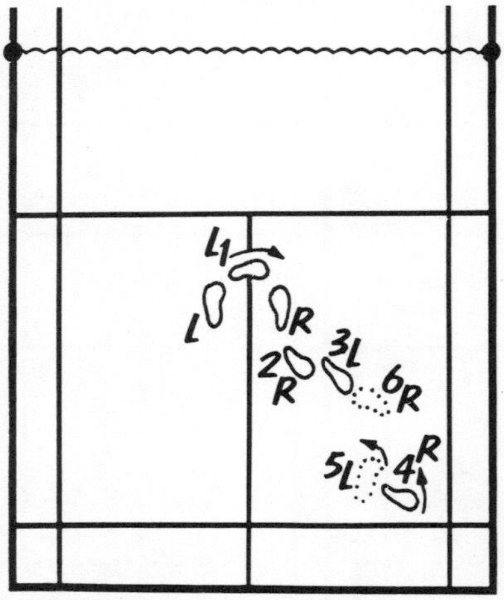

Figure 15

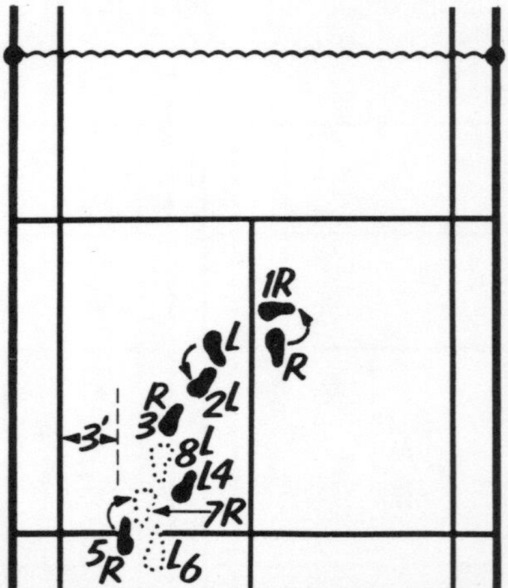

Figure 16

To return to the net (Figure 16, Steps 6-8) the left foot will be drawn up in a position parallel to the right foot and the body will pivot and turn clockwise to return toward the base with the right foot (Figure 16).

Movement to the sidelines is crucial to return smashes, intercept drives and to play half-courts.

Movement to the Right Sideline

One advantage of taking a very wide stance when anticipating a smash is that, from this position, the rising of one foot puts the body in motion in that direction. Thus taking advantage of gravitational forces, it provides impetus to the desired movement. As can be seen in Figure 17-a, the initial movement is to the right with the right foot. The distance covered with a powerful lunging move from the left leg, plus the outstretched racket, will allow the defender to reach within one foot of the alley. In order to move all the way to the sideline (as in doubles), a quick shuffle or chasse step (Figure 17-b) is needed so the player will still end up on the right foot for executing the return. In both instances, the player will push off from the right leg to return to the base position using opposite movement from the initial move.

Movement to the Left Sideline

This movement pattern requires more decision-making than the move to the right. In a situation where the shuttle has been hit very hard, but greater than one foot inside the sideline, the best move is to lift the left leg and lunge with the left foot as far as possible and

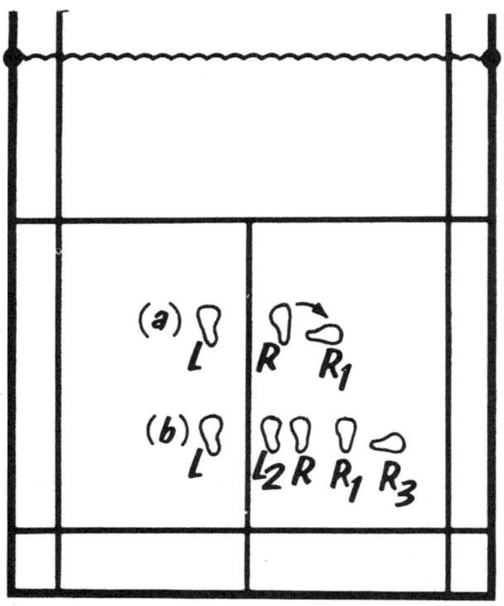

Figure 17

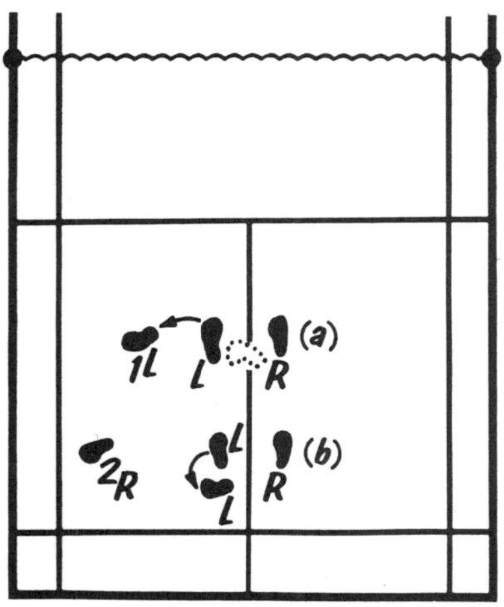

Figure 18

play a backhand return, making contact with the shuttle as far in front of the body as possible (Figure 18-a). This move gives less reach and the body is restricted in hitting shuttles that get past the side.

In retrieving shuttles hit farther from the body, but not quite so hard, the preferred movement pattern is the crossover step. The player will simultaneously push off the right leg and pivot the body counterclockwise and bring the left slightly to the right (Figure 18-b). The right leg will take a long step, moving the player as far as necessary to reach the shuttle. This latter movement pattern has the advantage of the swing not being restricted by the body, which would be the case if the last step were taken by the left leg. Photos BS2-BS3 illustrate the preferred unrestricted movement pattern for the crossover step. (See Page 31-32).

STRATEGY AND ANALYSIS OF THE GAME

Badminton is a game in which offense and defense change from side to side several times during a rally. Generally speaking, you are on the offense when you are hitting the shuttle downward (smashes, drops and half-court drives) or past your opponent (drives or attacking clears) into the deep corners of the court. Defensive shots are hit upward (clears) and give your opponent(s) opportunity to hit the shuttle downward (attack).

Drives are strokes that could be either offensive or defensive, depending upon court positioning. Play involving the hitting of many flat smashes and drives is called a "slashing" style of play. During these rallies neither side has established control of the rally and the players are battling on reflexes and quick racket movement until the offense can be taken. With players of equal ability, the player(s) maintaining the offense should win 60-80% of the rallies, but only 50% of the slashing type rallies.

Style of play often takes one of the following patterns:

1. Power Player — This style of play depends heavily on deep clears, fitness, and aggressive smashing ability. This person must be physically strong but could be less skilled in tactics, deceptive play and pin-point accuracy.
2. Runner — This style of play depends on the player's quick movement, fitness and agility in retrieving the opponents' shots. This style can be played by players without great power or finesse. The "runners" are generally good counterattackers who force their opponents out of position, rather than trying to force their openings by power.
3. Finesse Player — This style of play depends on the superb deceptive stroking ability of the player. The strategy is to maneuver the opponent out of position with quick, deceptive shots, and hit winning placements into the open area of the court. This player also depends on fitness, but may not have overpowering strength.

Many tournament players have the ability to play all three styles as this gives them flexibility in matching their opponents' style of play and game plan. It also gives the player the ability to change the pace and style of play if he is losing.

Singles Strategy

Singles is a game requiring control, patience and fitness. The general strategy is to maneuver your opponent out of the central areas of the court and force him to hit a weak return which you can hit for a point winner into the open area. Patience is needed because there will be many rapidly occurring opportunities for attack. Once on the attack, a player must have patience to choose the right time to go for the winner. In singles one cannot take himself out of position to hit a winner because if the shot is returned, the attack, most likely, will be reversed. One might liken patience to high percentage badminton. Play especially safe when your opponent is serving because the loss of the rally means the loss of a point. If you are serving, the loss of the rally is loss of service, but no points. Take your chances when you are serving.

Since the badminton court is 22 feet long, but only 17 feet wide, singles is a game of power to the deep corners and drops near the net. The ability of being able to control the depth of your shots is perhaps the most important and difficult aspect of most racket sports, and badminton is no exception. Certain knowledge of not having proper depth is that your opponent will be smashing a great deal and hitting drops which you cannot return in the forecourt.

To best control the tempo of the match and to keep the opponent off balance, one should have the opportunity to hit at least two different shots each time a shuttle is hit during a rally. Ideally, these two shots should be directed at opposite ends and sides of the opponent's court, which is 27.8 feet on the diagonal. This potential variety of placements will force the opponent to defend against shots requiring

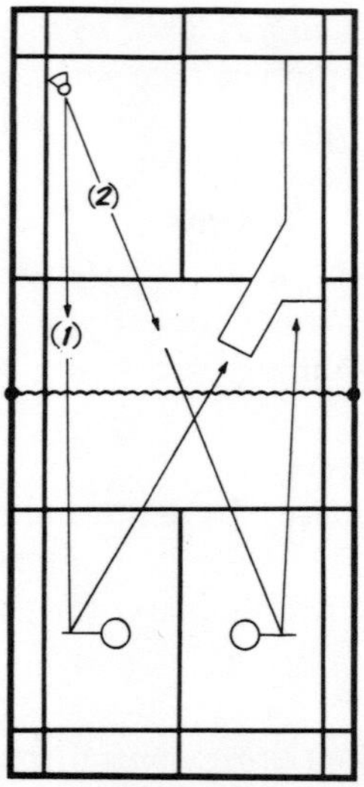

Figure 19

him to move the greatest distance from his base. Using this strategy, the attacker should be able to maintain the attack and control the rally.

The ability to change the direction of shuttle flight in badminton is one of the crucial aspects of singles strategy. To change direction, do the following: (1) if your opponent hits a shot straight over the net opposite you, return the shuttle cross-court, or (2) if your opponent hits a shot cross-court (diagonally) into your court, return the shuttle straight ahead (Figure 19). The importance of this strategy is that it makes your opponent run farther (cross-court) to return the shuttle. The opponent's straight-ahead shot should be returned cross-court about 50% of the time and 50% straight ahead. Often the cross-court return could be a more difficult shot and will require you to move cross-court to set your base for the next shot. The straight-ahead shot requires you to move less to reach a base for your opponent's next return.

There are two other advantages to changing direction when the opponents hit cross-court to you and good strategy would be to change direction by hitting a straight-ahead return about 90% of the time. First, the straight return of the shuttle is generally the simplest error-free shot to hit. Even a drive doesn't have much chance of being picked off or hit until it passes your opponent and is deep in the court. Second, the straight return gives you better positioning for your next shot since you will already be on the proper side of the court to set up your base. Try to think about this strategy. It makes your opponent run cross-court 60-75% of the time and also from the net to the back boundary line.

Play your opponent's back boundary line (baseline). One of the most effective singles strategies is to keep forcing your opponent back to his baseline. This is accomplished by hitting attacking clears, and pushing drives into the corner from the forecourt. This is particularly important for the following reasons:

1. It gives you time to get into position for the next shot.
2. It gives you more time to move to the shuttle after your opponent hits his shot.
3. It is more difficult and requires more energy by your opponent to move backwards than for you to move forward.
4. It takes more energy for your opponent to hit a shot from the baseline than for you to hit the shuttle from the net.
5. Keeping your opponent on the baseline will generally force him to hit more drop shots. If you can move forward quickly and catch the shuttle high, it may be possible to push another shot past your opponent who is in the process of moving forward to a base. This strategy often forces weak returns.

Once a person has been maneuvered out of position and gets to the shuttle late, good shot selection can keep him on the run. It is good strategy to try to maneuver an opponent farther and farther into a bad court position (away from the base position). This strategy is excellent against the "runners" because they need to be drawn way out of position in order for you to hit a winner against them. This type of play requires patience but is very effective.

When observing champion players it is very noticeable that all of their shots seem to be so easily and accurately executed. The mark of a champion is to always hit high percentage shots, that is, shots that can be executed without error. One of the reasons for this is that they are always in position to execute the shot they are trying to hit. All players should strive to hit shots that can be played safely (90% or greater chance to keep the shuttle in play without loss of court position).

In singles it is generally impossible to hide a weakness, especially if it is one of the 4 S's of badminton: Speed, Strength, Stamina or Stroking Skill.

A poor backhand is easily exploited when you are serving; however, with good shot selection and control you can keep exploitations of a weakness to a minimum. Hitting from your strength and controlling the game will help to prevent this.

In planning strategy the player should know what his best shot is. Ask yourself these questions: What shot do I hit that scores the most points? What shot do I hit that deceives my opponent? What shot do I hit best from each place on the court? Oddly enough, many players really don't know their best shots and how to set them up. For example, a player with deceptive and steeply angled smashes might try to set up this attack by trying to re-drop a drop shot the opponent hits from the back of the court. This re-drop might draw a shot clear off the net in which case the player can hit the straight-ahead or cross-court smash (his best shot).

There are many different combinations of shots that can help a player set up his point winner. These vary depending on the player's court position, shot-making skills, and speeds.

Most people are not strong enough to make openings with smashes. Smashing in singles is generally used to hit winning shots or as an element of surprise. The speed of the smash can be used against you if your opponent is in position to return the shuttle. In this case, the smasher has less time to get into position for the next shot. Smashing requires much more energy than other shots and can be very tiring if your opponent makes you run to hit your next shot.

Cross-court smashes are often a favorite shot of players. These smashes can be very deceptive and outright winners (cannot be returned), but if the opponent can get his racket to the shuttle, a straight-ahead block drop will get him out of trouble and reverse the attack. Good strategy is to use this one as a surprise shot (sparingly), or when your opponent has been drawn far out of position.

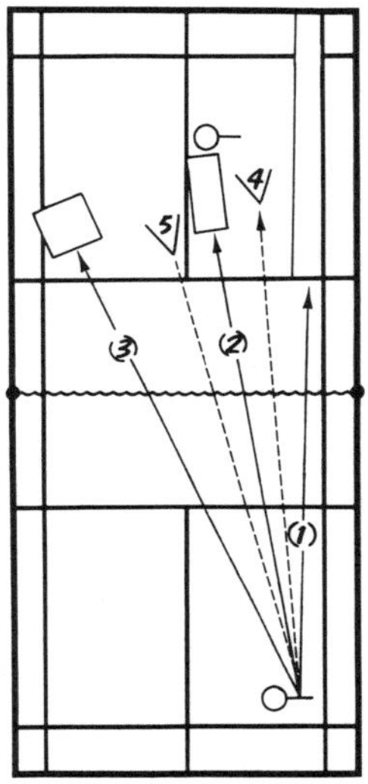

Figure 20

Effective use of the smash in singles when the shuttle is near one of the sidelines should be one of the following speed, direction and angle combinations. (See Figure 20):

1. Straight-ahead smash using a variety of speeds and angles.
2. Very **hard** smash directed at the opponent's body.
3. Cross-court smash hit off-speed with a quick deceptive motion, which should land between the short sevice line and a point about five feet deeper in the court as shown in the figure.

These three positions are the most difficult for your opponent to return. The straight-ahead and cross-court smashes could very well be winners. Usually the straight-ahead smash is preferable as it is safer and can be hit with a greater variety of speeds and angles and still be effective. The smash into the opponent's body should be returned, but with a weak shot generally in the middle forecourt, a position from which the smasher should be able to hit another smash or drop to win the rally.

Smashes hit off-target and directed into areas 4 and 5 of Figure 20 will generally enable the defender to play a safe return away from the smasher and reverse the attack.

If the smasher is hitting from near the center line, the smash could be directed down either sideline or right at the opponent's body.

Smashing accuracy from this location is not quite as important as from the sideline because the smasher is in better position to return the next shuttle should the opponent make a good return.

The most effective smash returns in singles are drives or drops directed cross-court from the smasher. Clears are also effective if they can be hit with good depth (near opponent's back boundary line) because the smasher is usually moving forward in anticipation of a weak return in the forecourt.

The cross-court smash must be mixed with power smashes at the opponent's body or straight down the sideline. In order to take full benefit of the good cross-court angle, it must be hit off-speed with a deceptive motion and land between the short service line and up to five feet deeper in the court. If it is hit harder, it will go out of the court (wide). See (Figure 20-3).

When you have the opportunity to hit smashes from the front two-thirds of the court, hard smashes directed at the opponent's body are very effective. When this occurs the opponent usually is cramped, having to hit the shuttle directed at his body and, thus, does not have power to hit hard drives or clears. This smash is generally returned with a block drop. Since the shuttle is hit at the opponent's body, the angle of return from the central areas of the court is poor. This strategy will allow the smasher to move into the forecourt (near the net) for a weak return and to hit a possible winner or controlling shot.

As badminton skills increase, the rallies become more fun, challenging and longer. Thus, more speed, stamina, strength, and skill will be required.

It is good strategy to keep some shots in your arsenal that your opponent has not seen you hit often. If you go all out with your most difficult, deceptive, spectacular and daring shots, your opponent will eventually become accustomed to these shots and start retrieving them. Thus, it is a good tactic to test out your opponent with a variety of shots early in the match to determine some specific weaknesses or stereotyped returns you might be able to capitalize on later. If the play is about even toward the end of the game, you may wish to hit some of these shots during the last two or three points of the game and then go back to your routine play until you need some points again.

All players must keep in mind that if your opponent has to run to the shuttle, you can usually glide smoothly about the court. If, on the other hand, you are scrambling, your opponent is probably gliding. The player having to scramble after shots will have less preparation for execution and come up with poorer (less accurate) shots, get more tired, and also eventually beaten.

How can we prevent the opponent from making us scramble about the court and from controlling the rallies? The best answer to this question is to start off the rally with a good serve or service return. There is really no excuse for missing the service or return of service because the rules dictate the shuttle cannot be served until both players are ready, and the serve is a defensive shot.

Singles Service

Service strategy has often been thought of as just getting the shuttle into play. However there is much more to it. This is one of your three most important shots, the return of service, and the put-away shot being the others. The service is a defensive shot since the shuttle must be hit over the five foot net from a position below the server's waist to the waiting opponent. However there are occasions when the service can actually be an offensive weapon, depending on both you and your opponent's strengths and weaknesses. Some of these situations will be discussed below.

Singles Service Stance

Position the body near the center line about 3-6 feet behind the short service line with the body facing the center of your opponent's court on a diagonal from you. (See Chapter IV for service stroking).

The most difficult service to return is the high, deep service that is falling straight down on your opponent's back boundary line. Since the shuttle is falling straight down, all attacking shots (smash, attacking clears and drops) must hit the feathers of the shuttle first, and thus greatly reduce the speed and accuracy of the return. This service is best returned with a loop drop shot or high, deep clear. It also draws the returner the maximum distance from his base position to make the return, which means he will have to move farther to reach a base for the next return. Attacking shots from this position are quite easily returned and often the attack is reversed due to the greater time the server has to move to the shuttle and hit from this deep position. This high, deep service coming down on the back line can also have psychological effects for the impatient player who likes to attack. First, he knows he cannot effectively attack his opponent, and second, the returner also knows his opponent knows he cannot attack effectively from this position. This high, deep shot coming straight down on the baseline is effective not only as a service, but at any time a player must go on the defense and has the power to hit the high, deep return. This shot is just like starting the rally all over again with a serve. It is safe from effective attack and will provide the player the most time to position himself for the next return.

As can be seen (Figure 21) for a right-handed player, the ideal service areas are (a) center of even court, and (b) any place on the baseline of the odd court. Serving to a right-handed player to the side baseline of the odd court can be very effective because the serve must be returned from a body position farthest from the base. This serve is especially effective against a player with less deceptive attacking clears and cross-court smashes.

The server will position himself in the center of the court for service returns hit from the center areas of the court (Figure 22). Note the player is equidistant from power shots (clears or smashes) that can be hit by his opponent.

When the serve is to the side baseline the best position for the server to take to narrow the angle of the return is to the side of the court from which the shuttle is being hit (Figure 23). The object is to move into position equidistant from the power shots (lines (1) and (2) in Figure 23). Although the player is farther from the path of an off-speed cross-court smash (line (3) in Figure 23), this shot allows the defender greater time to move to the shuttle than the others which must be defended first. Not only for service returns, but for all shots, the objective of the defender is to place himself equidistant from the power shots (quickest shuttles to be returned) that can be directed into his court. When expecting a clear or drop return, the player must also narrow the angle for front court and baseline movement possibilities.

Variation of Service Patterns

There are times when a variation in the high, deep service strategy

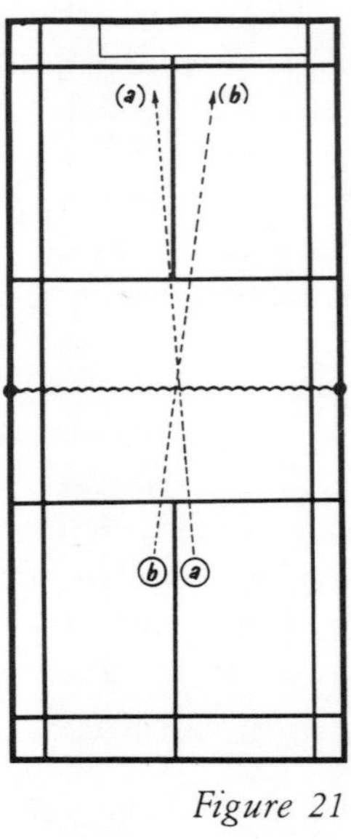

Figure 21

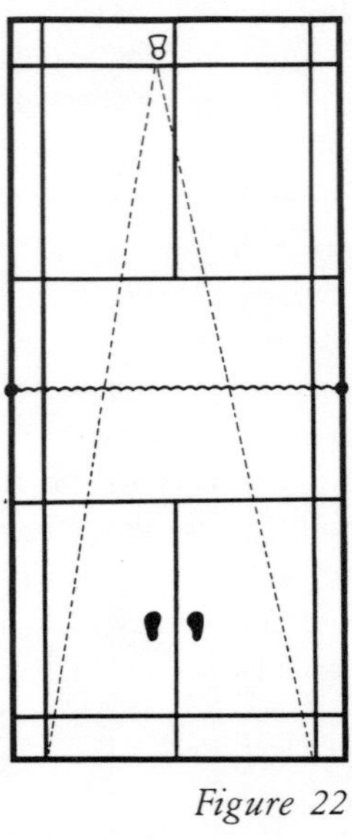

Figure 22

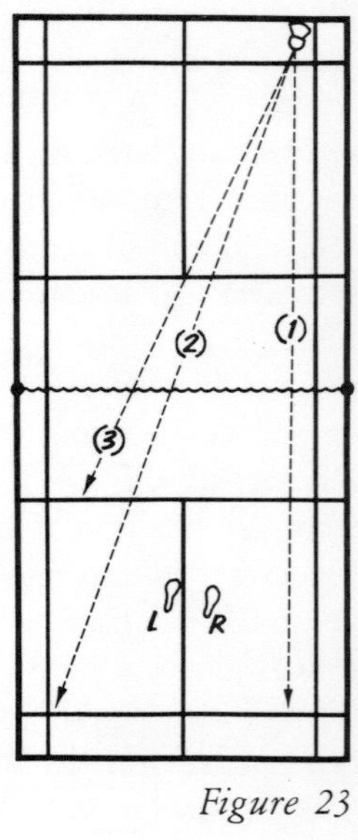

Figure 23

is necessary. Consider the following situations which might warrant a change:

1. Your opponent's deceptive drop and/or attacking clear combinations prevent you from regaining control of the rally.
2. You have served some shuttles out of court, or so short as to enable your opponent to put away the shuttle with a smash on the service return.
3. Your service seems to have good control, but several unforced errors don't let you get control of the rally.
4. Try other services to determine whether your opponent has good returns of these secondary serves.

Changing the trajectory of the deep service as well as varying placement between the center and side boundaries can be effective in preventing deceptive returns. This is very effective in keeping the service returner off balance, especially if he becomes a little lazy and doesn't hustle after the service. This lower trajectory service isn't recommended against tall opponents who generally have deceptive off-speed smashes because this player will intercept the shuttle in front of the long doubles service line and have the potential to hit a direct winner. As shown in Figure 24, the server has a wider angle to defend for these shots, which will also make him more susceptible to the attacking clear, also a favorite shot of most tall players with deceptive smashes.

The drive service, right at the opponent's chest, can be effective in singles against a player who does not have fast racket control. This service often restricts his stroking ability because the shuttle gets too

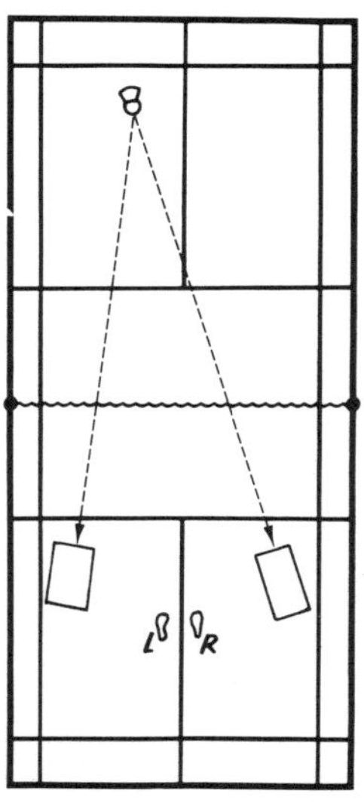

Figure 24

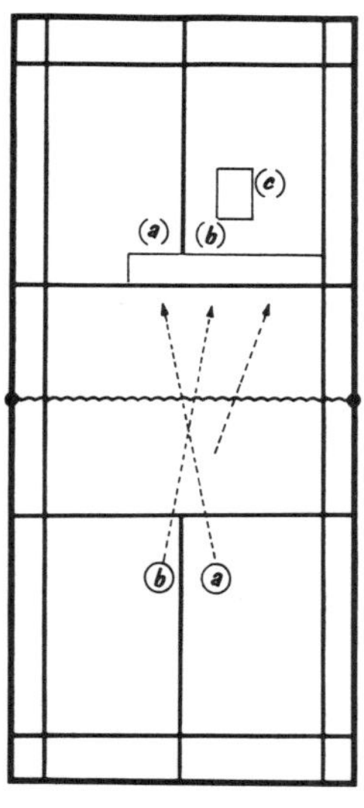

Figure 25

close to the body and cramps the swing. The drive service is not recommended for the quick-thinking player with a "quick racket" as the tempo is so fast the receiver can generally guide the shuttle into an unguarded area of the court before the server can determine the response.

The low, short service is often the first alternative to the high, deep service. When serving to the even court the prime target area is the center half of the court. (Figure 25-a). When serving to the odd court, the entire front of the court can be varied with about equal success (Figure 25-b). When a left-handed player is serving, the targets are the reverse of those shown in Figure 25. The advantage of the wide service is to pick off a low drive return and hit a cross-court smash for a winner. This is especially effective when a left-hander is serving the short, wide service to a right-hander in the even court and when a right-hander serves to a lefty in the odd court because the attempted drive service return off the forehand is easier to anticipate and the cross-court smash is into a slightly larger open court and on the backhand.

The low, short service is especially effective against the person who does not charge the service quickly, but lets the shuttle come to him. These people often hit high, deep clears which can be a safe and good return for this service. However, if this return strategy is used, the server should serve a low service that carries back into the service court about 4-6 feet. (See target area C in Figure 25 for this low service.) This slow charging player will then be cramped on the return and out of position for hitting accurate clears and drops. Thus, the server is likely to get the opportunity to smash a low clear or flat drive for an immediate advantage.

The return of the low service requires being alert, being in proper position, and making a quick movement to the net so as to intercept the shuttle near net tape height (as high as possible). The shot selection from intercepting the shuttle at this point can result in direct advantage for the receiver as he can hold drops to the corners or flick (drive) shuttles past the server into the baseline corners. The service return must also be hit from well in front of the short service line. A skilled short service returner will generally win these rallies in from one to three shots and quickly discourage his opponent from serving short.

The important service strategy here is that the server wants to get the short, low service dropping quickly over the net to the charging receiver and low and deep to the slow-charging player. This strategy takes away the receivers' best and favorite shots and forces them to hit secondary, less-practiced shots into your power.

One of the main advantages of the alternative to the high, deep service is that some players haven't practiced these service returns and come up with poor returns or sometimes get flustered and fail to get the shuttle in play at all (hit return out of the court or into net), thus giving away a free point.

Basic Service Returns

The most important shot in the rally for the service returner is the first one, the service return. In fact this may be considered the most important shot in badminton or probably any of the racket sports.

One often and most neglected aspect of returning the service is hustle and quick body movement to get into position for executing the return. Since the service must be hit over the 5-foot net and into the receiver's court, there is really no excuse for not executing a shot which will give the receiver the advantage and control of the rally. One cannot win in good competition if he does not take advantage by assuming the attack on the service return or gives away cheap points by hitting the shuttle out of court on this first shot.

A good serve return puts pressure on the server and should allow the receiver to maintain control of the rally with a variety of placements, thus keeping pressure on the server. Ultimately this strategy should result in winning most of the rallies when you are the receiver and prevent your opponent from scoring many points.

During the rally the service returner should not take chances or attempt spectacular low-percentage shots. An error here means the loss of a point. Good strategy is to take your chances and play your less-accurate shots when you need variety when you are the server. Thus, a bad error will not result in the loss of a point, but just a change of service.

Receiver Stance

Since the receiver will be moving either forward or backward to receive the serve, he should take a stance with the left foot forward about 1 foot from the center line and 4-5 feet behind the short service line (Figure 26-a) for the even court. In the odd court the player will be 3-4 feet to the left of the center line and 4-6 feet behind the short service line (Figure 26-b). If there is one time when a player hustles and concentrates most, it should be to return the service (both in singles and doubles events). This quick movement will prevent many return errors and give the receiver momentum for movement to the next shuttle.

Service Return Strategy

In order to keep the server at a base in the center of the court, there should be at least three good options available for each service return. To accomplish this best, there should be a shot at the net and one to the baseline to make the server potentially move the full length of the 22-foot court. There should be a shot to each sideline to make lateral movement also a maximum. The following service return alternatives are particularly effective in achieving this strategy. As shown in Figure 27 the straight-ahead attacking clear (1) and straight-ahead drop (2) will keep the player at about mid-depth in the court, but if too many shots are hit in these areas, the server will tend to move his base over a step (dotted circle) towards the sideline. In order to prevent this, an off-speed cross-court smash (3) will pull the server back into the normal base position and maybe a little forward. Although it is easier to point out this strategy for the service return, the players should have similar types of shot selection opportunities for most shots during a rally. A cross-court clear from this position on the court is a risky shot because it requires more power than most shots and, if it is hit a little low, it could be intercepted with a block drop over the net for a winner.

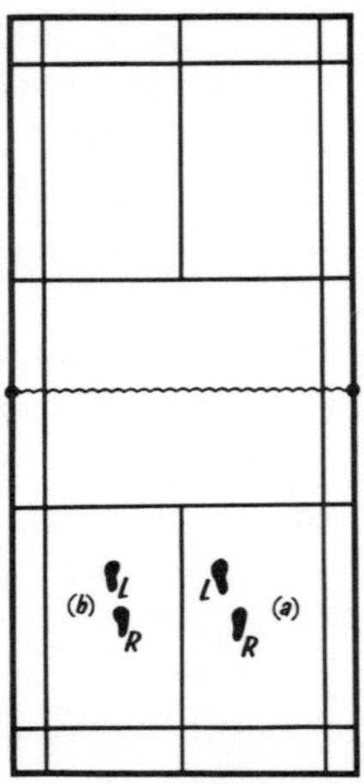

Figure 26

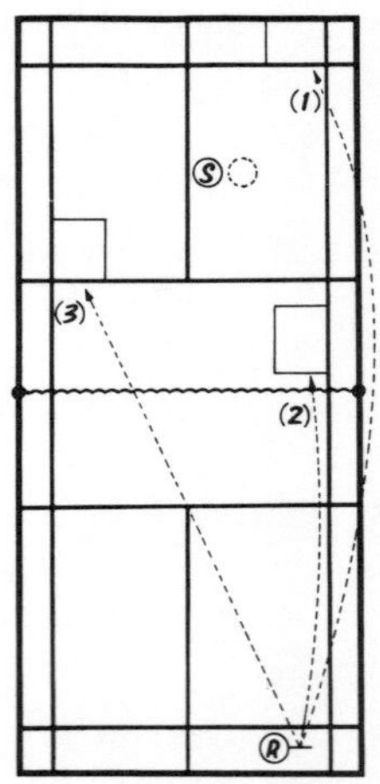

Figure 27

Short high serves should almost always be smashed, either down the sides or right at the racket side of the server's body (Figure 28A). When smashing the serve return, or other shots in singles, one must be careful not to hit the shuttle in areas about 2-4 feet on either side of the receiver's body. These smashes are all easily returned and the attack reversed with a block drop or cross-court drive. (Figure 28B)

Generally, at least half of the service returns should be clears and probably two-thirds or more clears and smashes during the rallies. The purpose of this strategy is to constantly keep pushing the shuttle deep into the corners and past your opponent. Retrieving these deep shots takes more energy than moving toward the net for drops. Opponents' shots hit from deep in the court will give you more time to play the returns.

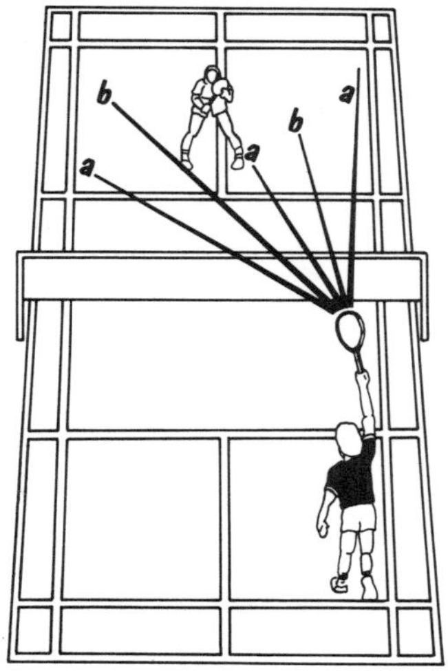

Figure 28

Varying the Direction of Play

Another basic tactic in playing singles is to try to make your opponent cover as much court as possible. This is accomplished by reversing the direction of flight to make your opponent move diagonally to retrieve the shuttle. If a shuttle is hit cross-court to you, your reply should be a straight-ahead shot at least 90% of the time. When your opponent hits straight ahead, your replies should be about 50% straight and 50% cross-court.

A frequent error in hitting straight-ahead drives to return a shuttle hit cross-court to you is to hit the shuttle wide. This is often due to neglect in considering the rebound effect of an object bouncing off the racket at the opposite angle from which it arrived (Figure 29). Thus, the racket hit should be perpendicular to a point about midway between the oncoming shuttle and the desired direction of return (Figure 29, dotted line).

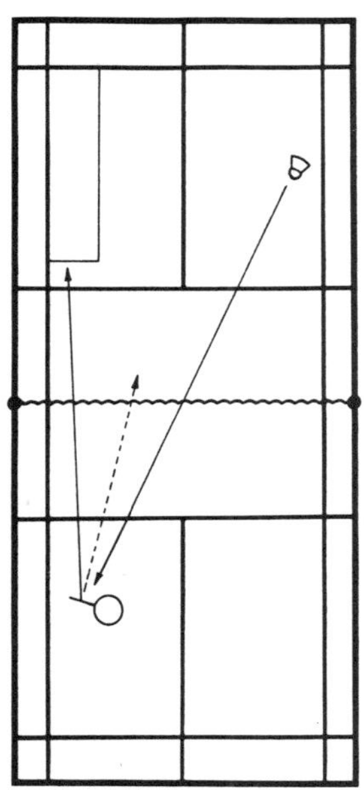

Figure 29

Varying the Tempo of the Game

A primary tactic to keep your opponent off balance is to change the speed of the game. This can be accomplished by two methods. First, work at a faster pace when you are winning rallies. Speed up the play by trying to shorten the time between rallies. On the other hand, if you are losing, you might want to slow the pace of the game by trying to lengthen these periods. The second method is to keep changing speeds of the shots. Smashes can be hit very hard, or fairly easy; clears can be hit very high or brought down to the level of attacking clears. Drives can be hit almost to the baseline or much easier in what we call a half-court shot (shuttle will land between the short service line and the middle of the court). Drops can be hit softly and very tight to the net, or harder with a flat trajectory which will carry back near the short service line or maybe even slightly deeper. Cut or slice shots will also effectively take place off the shuttle and change direction as well, thus adding deception to the play.

Some players feel indecision as to where to hit the shuttle. When in doubt, the high, deep clear is always a safe shot and one that will give you time to position yourself for the next return. However, there are certain shots that are best hit from various areas of the court. Figure 30 describes the repertoire of shots that are generally best hit from the various areas of the court as seen from the side and depicting a height and depth perspective.

Shots hit from the court areas marked in Figure 30 are listed below. Shots in parentheses are secondary alternatives.

A. Clears — Drops
B. Smashes (Drops)
C. Drives (Drops)
D. Clears (Drives)
E. Clears (Drops)
F. Drives — Clears (Drops)

For example, a shuttle struck in Section A should be cleared or dropped (area of basic service return or deep clear during a rally). Most shots in area B should be smashed. However, if your opponent is out of position, a drop could be effective also. Shots hit from area B are potential winners if the smash is used and the attack should hopefully not be relinquished. (Figure 30).

Methods of Practicing Singles

During the course of playing games in practice sessions, a player might want to concentrate on some of the play patterns, services and returns, attack and defense. This type of play is important because it occurs in fairly natural situations and your opponent doesn't have to

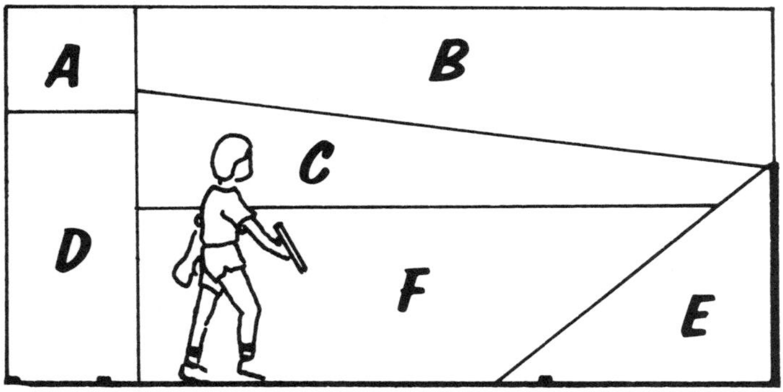

Figure 30

know what you are doing and thus cannot overplay your shots (practice various styles of play).

Some of these patterns and styles are:

1. Try to alternate between clears and drops regardless of opponent's shots.
2. Try to hit two clears to one drop.
3. Play the entire game using only the straight-ahead attacking clear, or some other return of the high, deep service.
4. Serve only low serves, or wide serves, or drive serves.
5. Try to play defense and look for opportunities to counterattack.
6. Play an attacking and smashing game for all clears.
7. Concentrate on changing direction of all cross-court shots.

Doubles Strategy (Ladies and Men)

Ladies' and men's doubles are quite similar in strategy, positioning and shot selection. However, women, usually having less power, will generally hit more drops and clears to maneuver their opponents out of position before smashing to win the rally. Men usually stand closer to the service line when returning the serve and thus put more pressure on the server right from the beginning of the rally.

Since there are two players to cover the court, doubles strategy emphasizes the attack and smashing more than singles. The rallies generally start with a low service because the depth of the service court is 2½ feet shorter than in singles, followed by a series of low, flat shots. These rallies become a game of "cat and mouse" with clever deceptive shots, drops, half-court drives and drives, until one team is forced to lift the shuttle (clear). When this occurs, the opposing team gains the attack and has the opportunity to hit a smash.

Once on the offense, good strategy (teamwork and shot selection) should enable them to maintain the attack and eventually to win the rally. Once a team has gained the advantage and has the potential to smash, they should rotate into the attacking position and their opponents should take a defensive position so as to be able to defend their court. Teams can move about the court attacking, defending and reversing the attack many times during the course of rally. The teamwork employed in alternating between offensive and defensive court positions is called the "rotational system" and is used by all tournament players. Once on the offense, however, a strategy employing good teamwork and shot selection should enable the attackers to keep pressure on their opponents and eventually win the rally.

The Attacking Formation

The primary attacking position is one in which one player is in position to smash the shuttle, usually from deep in the court, and the partner takes a position to put away any weak returns which are most likely to occur in the mid- or forecourts.

Note front player is well behind the short service line.

This is often called the up and back position.

The Defensive Formation

Since a smash is the primary weapon of the attacking team, the defenders must be able to defend the entire width of their court. A team playing in the up and back formation (offensive) can seldom cover both sidelines against the smash. Thus, the best defense is achieved by taking a position side by side, halfway between the net and baseline. (See photo above).

Tandem Movement Patterns

Both the attacking and defending teams will move about the court in tandem, depending on where the shuttle is located.

The basic strategy of doubles is to play shots which will allow you to get in the attacking position and thus control the rally. Once in the attacking position, the primary shots should be smashes and the secondary shots are drops and half-court drives since the trajectory of these shots will force the opponents to defend with shots hit from below net tape level. This strategy in shot selection forces the defense to lift the shuttle so the attack can be maintained.

The strategy of the defending team is to try to reverse the attack by hitting flat drives or drops away from the attackers. Thus, the offensive team will be unable to hit another smash. When this occurs, there is usually another series of shots in which both teams are in the attacking position and hit drives and half-courts until one team is forced to clear the shuttle and go on the defense. A poorly placed offensive shot can be returned by a strategically placed shot to give an outright winner or force a defensive shot (clear). Thus, sometimes a team on defense can completely reverse the attack with one well-placed shot.

Smashing

In doubles, the smasher must consider the three most important aspects of the stroke: (a) direction or placement, (b) angle, and (c) speed. In addition, the backcourt smasher must always remember that his job is to force his opponents to return a weak shot in the front and mid-court region so his partner can hit the winning shot. A serious error is to think you are going to hit a winner by smashing from the backcourt.

A. Direction: As shown by direction (1) in Figure 31, the primary

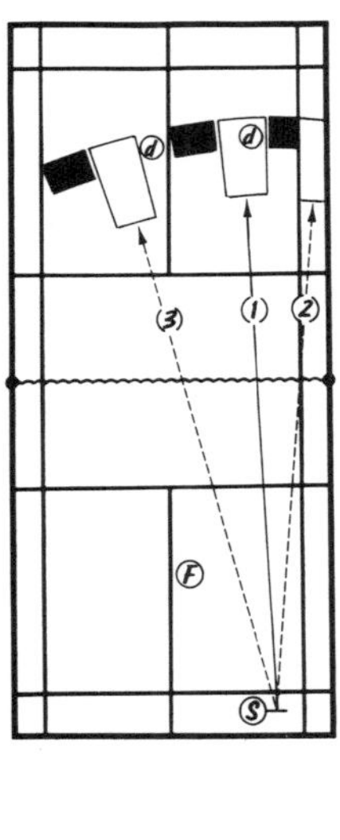

Figure 31

smashing direction is at the player directly across from the smasher, and to the inside (the target is about three feet wide). From this position the defender's return is most likely to be hit within reach of your partner positioned in the midcourt region in front of the smasher.

The primary secondary target area is directed toward the alley of the player in front of the smasher (dotted line (2) in Figure 31). This shot is effective when the shots down the middle tend to draw attention away from the alley smash. The smash should have good speed and steep angle to prevent a cross-court drive by the defender. Another secondary target area (dotted line (3) in Figure 31) is to smash to the cross-court player on the defender's right hand side. This smash keeps the cross-court defender from helping out with the primary smashes toward the center of the court and is generally a safe shot because the defender must swing back toward the oncoming shuttle in a slightly cramped position. It is difficult for the defender to block or drive this shuttle down the left hand alley of the attacking team, although this is the desired defender's return shot as it will reverse the attack.

The shaded areas of Figure 31 are poor areas to smash the shuttle because the receivers can hit drives and blocks away from the attacking team and reverse the attack.

B. Smashing Angle: The angle of the smash is an important variable in smashing effectiveness. If the shuttle can be hit from a position high above the smasher's head and angled steeply downward to just pass over the net, by the time it approaches the defender it is below the defender's knees. From this position the attacking team has an excellent opportunity to keep the pressure on the defensive team and continue smashing. Generally, the closer the smasher is to the net, the better (steeper) the angle of the smash. As skills develop, many doubles players will jump in the air to get better angle on their smashes. Smashes that are hit flat (not angled downward) are easily blocked off or driven toward the sidelines and can be directed away from the attacking front court player. Poorly angled smashes will make it difficult for the attacking team to keep the offense.

C. Smashing Speed: Most people like to smash the shuttle as hard as they can and if the attacking team is on balance in good tactical position, a very hard smash is the most effective weapon. However, if the defensive team is ready, a hard smash directed to a bad position or with a poor angle can lead to a quick reversal in the attack. In order to keep the defense off balance and unsure of the timing, it is an excellent tactic to hit smashes of varying speeds. The cut-smash is particularly effective because (1) it is often difficult to detect the direction in which it is being hit, (2) the defender often has to move forward since this smash has greater angle and (3) the defender must swing harder in order to return the shuttle. These factors also give the front court player (smasher's partner) more cues and time to anticipate and intercept the opponent's return. Another difficult smash to return is an off-speed smash directed about chest-high right at the defender's body. This smash often cramps the defender's stroking and leads to a weak return in the middle area of the court.

The smasher's effectiveness can be evaluated by observing the play of the front court player. If the front court player is hitting lots of winning shots, the smasher has done a good job. In a like manner, if the front court player is making several errors and fails to keep the attack, the smasher has probably been off target with the smashes.

Role of the Front Court Player (Smasher's Partner)

The tactics of the front court doubles player are essential to winning and are also least understood by most teams. This player may only hit one or two shots in a long rally, but must be ready to pick off the weak return to finish off the rally (win the point). This person must constantly be moving in order to accomplish the following duties:

1. **Prevent a drop return.** Any drops that are returned must be met above net level if possible, thus giving the potential to hit a winning shot. The strategy of the front person is to be positioned as deeply as possible so as to invite a drop return by the opponent which can be put away with a quick step, lunge and smash at the net. This is the "sucker" play in badminton. Being far back in the court will also give the front court player more opportunities to

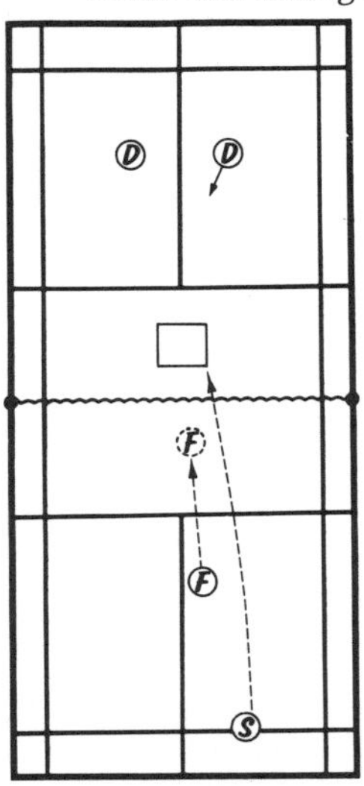

Figure 32

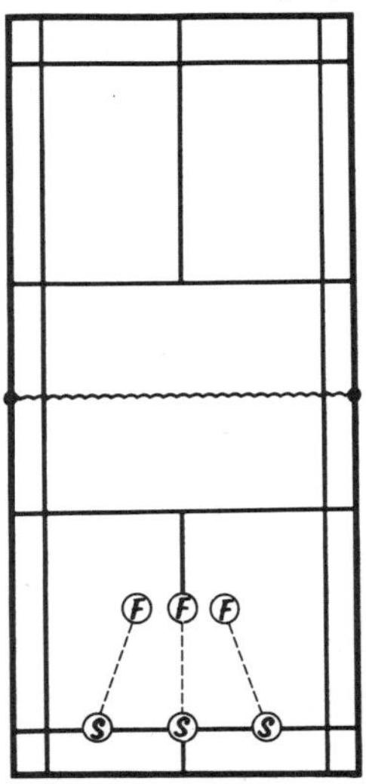

Figure 33

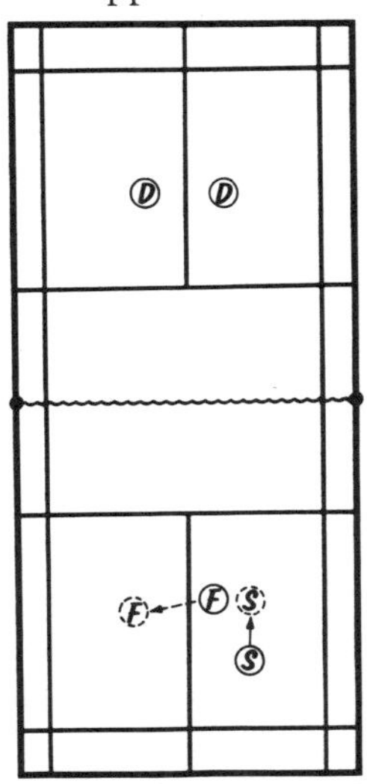

Figure 34

intercept weak drives or short clears, thus maintaining the pressure of the attack.

If the smasher hits a drop instead of a smash, the front court player must react quickly by moving up in the court (even in front of the short service line) to prevent the re-drop (Figure 32). A re-drop by the defenders will immediately reverse the attack, thus the only shot the front court player anticipates in this case is a re-drop. This is accomplished by proper positioning and usually not by hitting the shuttle. All other shots can be returned by the backcourt player who should hit a smash (preferably) or control shot.

2. **Move in tandem.** The front court player must move in tandem with the smasher in order to be in position to cut off the shuttle and hit a winning smash. Some tandem formations are shown in Figure 33. Note the depth of the front court player which is often 4-8 feet behind the short service line. He is seldom at the "T" if his partner can smash. This is the ideal position for the front court player because (a) there is more time to play the shuttle in front of the body, (b) the player will not have to move backward to cover areas of the court and (c) he will get more action from this part of the court.

   As shown in Figure 34, if the smasher hits a shuttle from farther up in the court, the front court player will quickly rotate to the opposite side of the court, and each player covers for the weak return which would be expected from a smash from this area. Quick movement by the front player is important because there is less confusion as to who hits the shot and visibility is not restricted. Often players will call "yours" or "mine," so as to indicate who will hit this smash.

   It is important strategy for the front court player to move quickly to the same side of the court from which the shuttle is being hit, regardless of whether his partner or opponent is hitting the shuttle. From this position the front court player has more opportunities to intercept weak returns and take the offense.

3. **Know when to cut.** The front court player must know which shuttles to let go and which to hit. When the defenders hit a hard drive about net height, there is a tendency for the front court player to try to hit it. This swing often results in an error. The front court player must try to play only returns from in front of the body, rather than to the side. It is generally better to let the drive be returned by the smasher (backcourt player), who should have recovered from hitting the smash and should be able to direct a drop or half-court shot away from the opponents to maintain the attack.

4. **Finishing off the rally.** Once the front court player has a chance to hit a shuttle, he must keep pressure on the defense and win the rally within 2-4 shots. One of the best tactics is to hit the first one or two shots into the body of the defender and also keep moving forward toward the net for a quick smash aimed right at the center line, or possibly a half-court block away from the defender and directed toward the singles sidelines. The tactic of punching the shuttle at the defender's body is important because the angle of return will be directed back to the front court attacker. Shots that come very close to the net will often be hit with a "brush" shot (see reverse cut Pg. 26) which reduces the speed and keeps the shuttle from going out the back of the court and prevents the follow-through of the swing from striking the net.

Defensive Strategy

All players must know how to play defense, although it is better to be on the attack. Thus, the strategy of the defending team is to reverse the attack. Helpful tactics to improve defensive play are discussed below.

Court Coverage

The basic methods of doubles court coverage are to (a) keep both players equidistant from the smasher, (b) play a backhand defense and (c) defend the center of the court by the player who is cross-court from the smasher. Figure 35 depicts the basic defensive position when a smash can be hit from the deep left baseline. Player A must defend all smashes to the left of the dotted line shown between the two players with Players B defending the rest of the court. The best returns are deep and half-court drives, deep clears, and well-directed drops away from the attackers. (See photo)

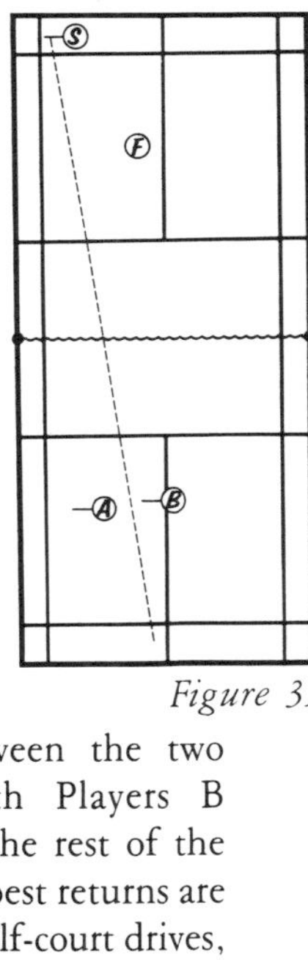

Figure 35

It is best to try to make the attacking team run as far as possible to hit the next shuttle. This tactic makes them both move and change positions, requires more energy, and makes it more difficult to execute well-placed and hard smashes when on the move and perhaps off balance. Figure 36 depicts the basic targets the defensive team would like to hit on the smash return. These are drives, half-courts and blocks.

It is generally easier to defend from the backhand, so players will position themselves for backhand returns when possible. Right-handed players will usually defend better in the left (odd court) so if they are forced to hit a clear, they should try to run their opponents into the deep even court (position shown in Figure 36). If they are able to execute a defensive cross-court shot, the attacker will have to chase the shuttle to the backhand side. Left-handed players will probably defend better on the right (even) court.

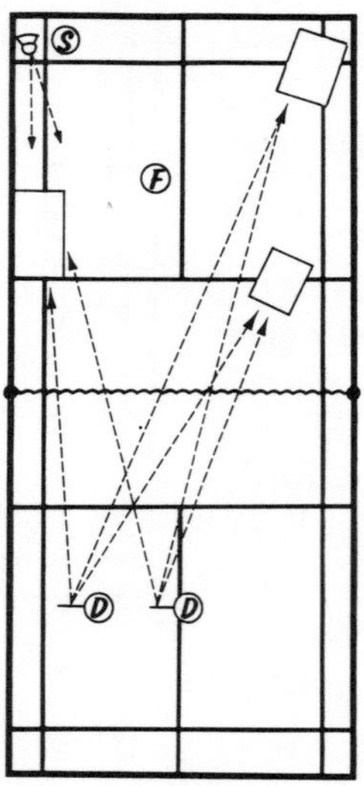

Figure 36

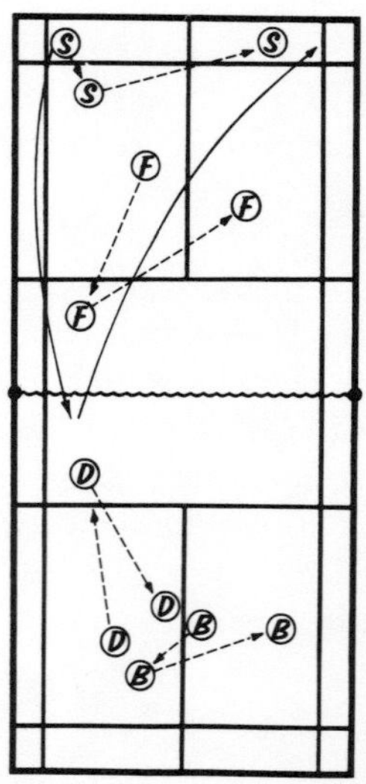

Figure 37

If a player must clear a drop and go on the defense, it is generally better to clear the shuttle cross-court to the deep sideline in front of his partner. This tactic will run the attackers into the corner and his partner, who should already be in good position, will most likely be required to return the smash (Figure 37).

Figure 37 shows the typical movement pattern and court coverage of the attacking and defensive teams. The attacker (Player S) hits a drop which defensive Player D will retrieve and clear cross-court. The attacking front court player (Player F) will move to the net to prevent Player D from hitting a re-drop, thus leaving the cross-court vulnerable. When Player D moves to retrieve the drop, his partner (Player B) moves to the left to protect the backcourt and perhaps go on the offense if Player D can safely re-drop. Since there was a clear, Player B must move to defend against a possible smash in the right court. Player D will retreat to a base position near the center line. The attacking Player S must move quickly to the backhand corner in an attempt to hit another attacking shuttle. If Player D were able to move very quickly to the net and catch the shuttle high, he might be able to execute an attacking clear or drive cross-court which would most likely reverse the attack. This is why most of the shots from the attacking position should be smashes. However, if drops are to be hit, placement to the center of the court may cause confusion as to which defensive player will retrieve it and, more importantly, prevent a well-angled return to the corners — thus making it easier to maintain the attack. The only problem with the drop to the middle is that one of the two players may anticipate a drop and move in for the kill or at least reverse the attack with a quick re-drop or drive.

Defending against the smash hit from the deep center court areas is most difficult (Figure 38). The defenders need to play at about equal depth and in the center of their respective sides. They have poor angles in which to target drives so must hit low, hard flat returns or clears to the baseline corners. To avoid this position, it is important to keep clears directed toward the corners.

A good defensive tactic is to never clear the shuttle right back to the smasher and give him the chance of smashing again. If the attacker has two or three smashes in succession, he should be able to draw a

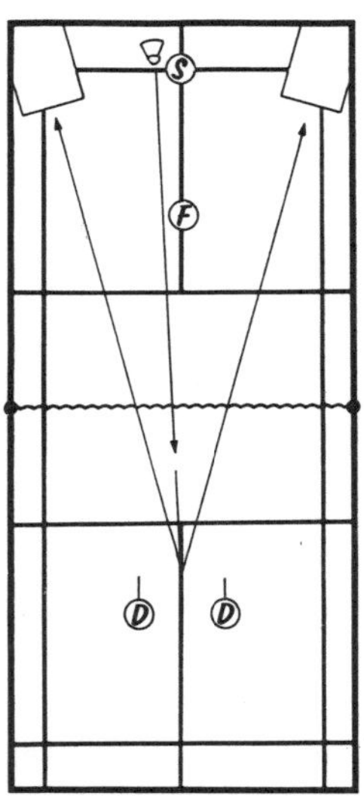

Figure 38

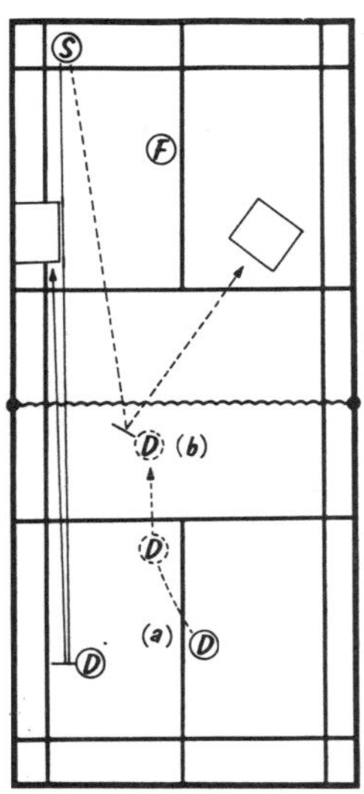

Figure 39

weak return for his partner to kill at the net.

The cross-court defender has an interesting role in doubles. This person has much more flexibility and can sometimes help out his partner. The cross-court player can often determine that the attacker is not going to hit the shuttle on his side of the court. When this split-second judgment occurs, the player should break toward the net. This can be advantageous if his partner hits a good drive or block (Figure 39-a); they will very quickly be in the attacking position. If the attacker hits a drop, the player can often retrieve it for his partner and also reverse the attack (Figure 39-b). Thus, it is good for the smasher to attack this potentially overzealous cross-court defender if he tries to anticipate too much.

Slashing Rallies

In the heat of play, there is a tendency for players to find themselves hitting a series of hard drives called "slashing rallies." To the spectator these rallies are wild, spectacular and most exciting. Both teams have an equal chance of winning them, whereas a team gaining the attack and hitting well-placed shots should win about 70% of the rallies.

How does one get from the slashing rally to the smashing position? The best method of gaining the attack is to hit a half-court down one of the sidelines. The most difficult part of this tactic is realizing the half-court shot should be hit in the midst of an exciting and fun rally.

As players become more experienced and used to partnering a certain player, they will begin to have a feel of where their partner is going to hit the shuttle and of which returns are most successful and taking advantage of the strength of the team. It is advantageous to be on the offense with the powerful smasher in the backcourt, rather than at the net. Clever teamwork can accomplish this goal. For example, this position can be accomplished by (a) all deep shots in the middle area of the court are hit by the power player, and/or (b) all drops will be followed to the forecourt by the net player and the smasher will move to the backcourt.

In doubles there are two basic play patterns. First, the offensive versus defensive play pattern, in which the offensive team is in the up and back formation and the defensive team plays side by side and tries he attack by hitting the shuttle down the sides and away ttackers. (Photo Pg. 70)

econd play pattern occurs when both teams are in the offensive position, but neither team has forced the other to lift the shuttle so they can attack with a smash. Thus the shots are drives, half-court shots and net play. Players on the defensive team will move into this potential attack formation when one player tries to reverse the attack in hitting a drive, half-court drive or drop shot. Both teams will also be in the offensive formation to begin the rally from the service and return of service positions. Some people liken these patterns to a "cat and mouse" play where one team tries to out-finesse their opponents and force them to take a defensive position.

Doubles Service and Service Return Strategy

The basic service positions are shown in Figure 40. The server will usually stand close to the center line and (a) close to the short service line when delivering the backhand service, or (b) from 1-3 feet behind the short service line when using the forehand service. The server's partner will straddle the center line about 8-10 feet behind the short service line (3-5 feet in front of the long doubles service line). Thus, when serving, they are in an offensive formation (up and back).

The Role of the Server

The prime objective in serving is to get a rally started and to prevent the receiving team from controlling it. High, deep serves will provide the serve returner the opportunity to attack by smashing the service, thus low, short serves are preferable. The three target areas for the short serve are shown in Figure 40 when serving to right-handers in the even court, and Figure 41 for serving into the odd court.

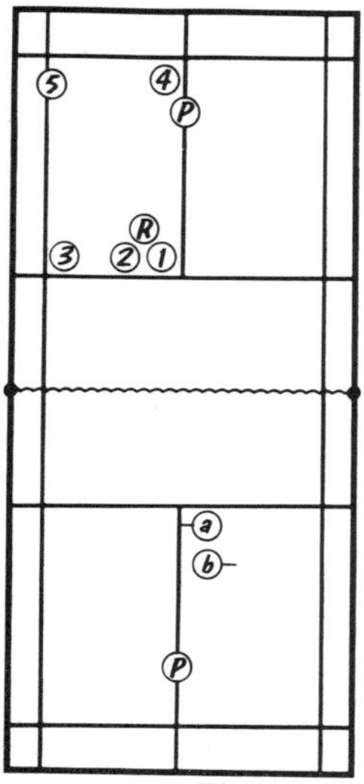

Figure 40

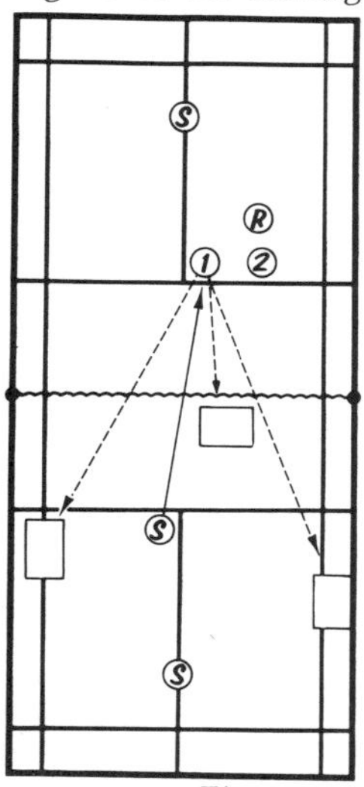

Figure 41

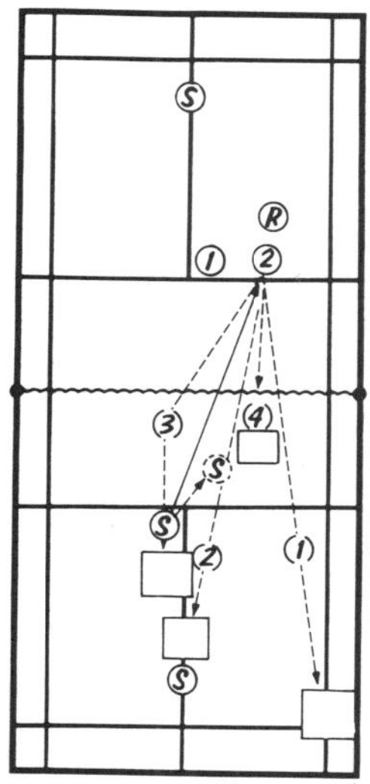

Figure 42

The service to the "T" (1), or to the receiver's right shoulder (2), are the primary services and the frequency of each depends on the returner's selection of serve returns. Service returns from the "T" position as depicted in Figure 41 by the dotted lines to the half-court positions and drops to the net are very effective against this serve. Serve returners who are not well-skilled in hitting these shots should be served to the "T." Players who are skilled in half-court returns should be served into the body (see (2) in Figure 42) since it is difficult to hit half-courts from this position. These serves force one of the following four returns: (1) hard and flat drives deep into the corner, (2) drives into the body of the server's partner, (3) a soft shot just over the server's head or (4) a net drop. Most players are better skilled in returns of one of these major types of serves than the other: serves to the "T" or serves directed at their body. The server must determine the returner's weakness and serve to this position. If the returner starts to overplay certain returns, the server should vary the service with wide, flick or drive serves (Figure 40-3, 4, or 5).

After determining where to serve to the opponents, the server must prevent the drop returns. After hitting the service, the server must step in front of the returner or follow the direction of the service (note server's movement in Figure 42). Should the returner hit a drop, the server should be able to play a smash or brush shot by meeting the shuttle above the net. This prevention of the drop service return is crucial to winning doubles and preserving the opportunity of maintaining the attack and winning the rallies. This quick move by the server will also force the returner to put more pace on the shuttle to prevent the server from intercepting it. This tactic will generally give the server's partner a better chance to intercept the shuttle with an attacking shot.

Although a good drop shot service return will force a defensive clear and gain the attack for the receiver, this is a dangerous return against a good server. The service returners should not depend on the drop return as their best and most reliable return because the server should be able to nullify this return with good net play.

Once the server has established the role of dominating the net (preventing drop returns), he should begin to look for service return patterns and be prepared to anticipate a half-court return when an important point is needed.

The server uses flick and drive serves to vary the tempo of the game and to prevent the serve returner from overanticipating the low service. Use the low, wide service or drive or flick service if you have made some good services but have failed to score any points, your opponents are making great returns, or if you or your partner make some unforced errors. The low wide, flick and drive serves will at least change the play patterns, and maybe in the server's favor. It is good strategy to try out some flick and drive serves early in the match or scout your opponents to know what type of returns they are likely to hit.

Sometimes in ladies' doubles, the server may use a high, deep service directed toward the sideline and let the receivers have the attack.

The servers will have plenty of time to take their desired defensive position and, against opponents with less power, wait patiently to reverse the attack which also tends to force them out of a good defensive position. This counter-attacking service strategy is seldom used in men's doubles due to the more powerful smashes and the threat of hitting a service return winner.

A rarely used service formation is (Figure 43) where the right-handed server moves to the right alley and serves a drive into the right-handed receiver's deep center court (backhand). This service can be effective against weak or inexperienced players or might be a good change of pace because it is rarely practiced. The strategy is to attack the backhand, so this serve is not effective against left-handers in the even court, or right-handers in the odd court. The disadvantage of this service is that the servers are not in the attacking position and a drop between the serving team players will automatically give the receiving team the attack (Figure 43).

The Techniques of Returning the Service

While the service team is attempting to get a rally going, the basic strategy of the receiving team should be to force the attack and try to win the rally in 2-4 shots. The service receiver will take a position someplace within 3 feet of the short service line (Figure 44). As can be seen in Figure 44, in the even court (solid line) the players should be positioned about 1-1½ feet from the centerline to prevent a drive down the backhand (center) and, while receiving in the odd court (dot-

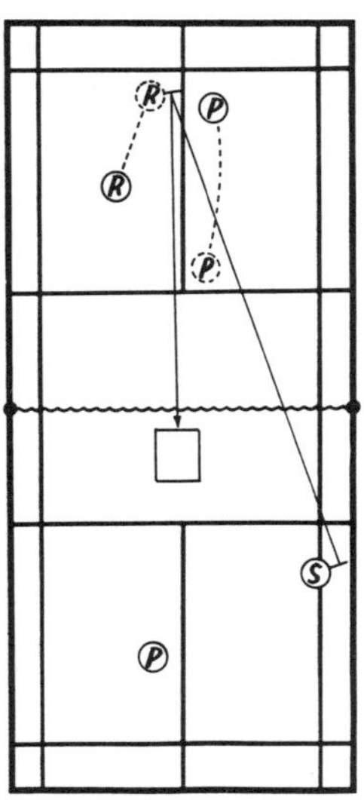

Figure 43

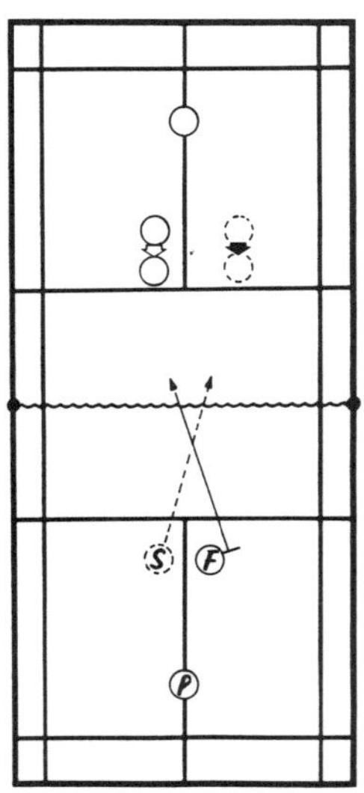

Figure 44

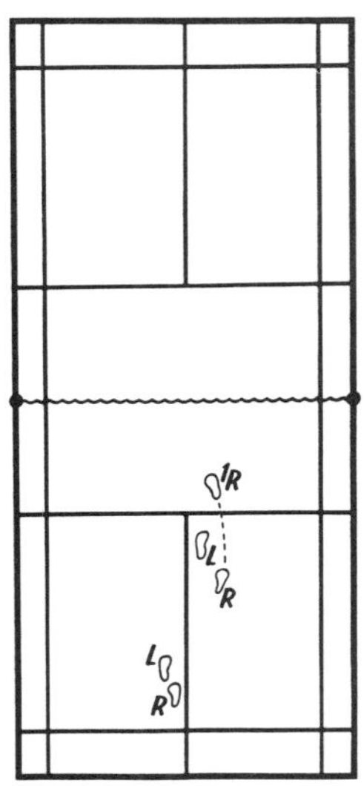

Figure 45

ted lines) play 3-4 feet from the centerline. As skill increases, players will stand closer to the short service line when receiving the service (arrows in Fig. 44). The general rule is to stand as close as possible to the short service line to put pressure on the server, and yet be able to move backward quickly enough to smash all flick and drive serves.

The service returner should use the following technique to effectively rush the short, low service. Taking a position with the left foot forward, and at the instant the receiver can determine a short, low serve is being hit, the first move is a quickly executed cross-over step and lunge with the right leg (Figure 45). The second part of the movement pattern is the stroking of the shuttle. During the cross-over step and lunge, the right shoulder will rotate clockwise and the arm will enter in front of the body toward the oncoming shuttle. With this forward movement, the head of the racket will automatically be cocked back, thus, the racket is not taken back for a backswing.

By this time in the movement pattern, the returner should know exactly where the shuttle will be intercepted and, leading with the right elbow in front of the body, either forehand or backhand returns can be hit. The hitting of the shuttle will be accomplished by forearm rotation and wrist flexion from the forehand or backhand position.

This technique is important and one should not be committed to hit a hard return during the cross-over step. The brush shot is often used to make a deceptive swing and reduce power to keep the shuttle from going out the end of the court (follow-through is to the left side of the body, with the face of the racket remaining parallel to the net).

Using the cross-over step and lunge techniques, the serve returner's best options for returning the short, low service are (1) half-court shots into the alleys, (2) drives into the body of the server's partner, (3) drops and (4) push shots just over the server's head (Figure 41-42). Clears are poor options since the server's partner is in position to smash this shot.

To return a flick or drive service, the server returner should try to hit a sharply angled smash (1) straight into the body of the server, (2) down the sideline or (3) into the body of the server's partner (Figure 46). Similar returns are also hit when the service flick or drive is directed toward the sideline. The following movement technique is used to intercept the deep doubles service.

From the basic service return position (Figure 47), with the left leg forward, the player will push and step backward from the left leg (step 1) to the right leg (step 2). From this position he will make a powerful jump toward the shuttle off the right leg and (with a counterclockwise) rotation of the body, extension of the arm, inward rotation of the

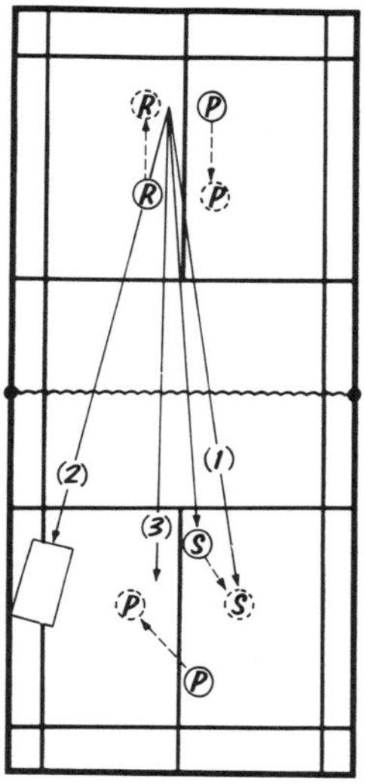

Figure 46

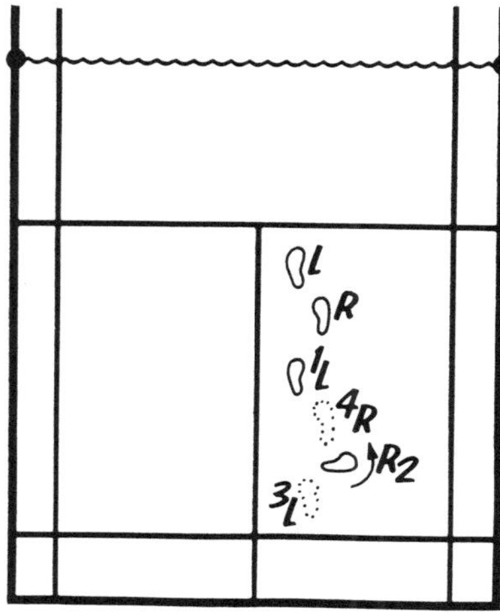

Figure 47

forearm and flexion of the wrist) smash the shuttle from this airborne position. The left leg will catch the body (step 3) and, with continued rotation, a step forward with the right leg (step 4) will move the player back toward the base position. Note in Figure 46 that the returner's partner (P) moves into the front court position when the deep service is hit, and he should, ideally, be there before the serve return is hit.

The serving team has two options for playing the receiver's return. First, as shown in Figure 46, a side-by-side defense can be set up (P and S positions), but this has the disadvantage in that (1) the smash may be hit before the servers are able to move into position for the defense and (2) they are vulnerable for a drop since the server is backing up. Generally, a better strategy is for the server to remain in the front court to anticipate a drop shot return, and the server's partner to be responsible for covering the entire width of the court against the smash. This may seem like a big task, but if the server only occasionally uses the flick or drive serve, the returner will usually be caught off-balance and unable to direct a smash down one of the alleys, the only return the server's partner will be unable to control.

The role of both the server and receiver's partner is to smash all shuttles that are lifted above their heads in the backcourt or to play half-court drives and drops away from the opposing forecourt player. Thus, the rally will proceed on the ''cat and mouse'' basis until some player is able to hit a shot to force the opposing team to lift the shuttle and take a defensive position.

In summary, the basic strategy of doubles is for both teams to begin the rally in the offensive court positions and play "cat and mouse" until one team is forced to lift the shuttle and take a defensive position and defend against the smash. Once a team is able to smash, the other team tries to defend with a drive, half-court or drop to get back into a "cat and mouse" rally and then fight for the attack by forcing the opponents to lift the shuttle.

Mixed Doubles Strategy

Mixed doubles strategy is very similar to the "cat and mouse" type play of doubles, except the players are usually positioned with the female in the forecourt and the male in the backcourt. Most teams rarely lift the shuttle and/or move into a side-by-side defensive position. Instead, they try more risky drop, half-court or drive shots rather than lift the shuttle so the man can smash at the woman. Although many women are good defenders, the man will have the advantage when smashing against the woman. Some teams will stay in the up and back offensive formation when the opponents are smashing and hope the backcourt player will be able to half-court or drive return the first smash and thus take the attack away. However, if the smasher can be accurate enough to direct a smash into one of the alleys, it will almost always win the rally against this defense.

Most mixed teams will defend the smash by having the woman take a position cross-court from the smasher about 1-2 feet behind the short service line. (See photo below.)

The objective is to block the smash into the open court away from the smasher (Figure 48). In this defensive formation the man will return all clears, drops, and smashes in the straight-ahead court from the smasher and the cross-court attacking clear over the woman's head (shaded areas of court in Figure 48).

A major weakness of this defense is that the straight-ahead drop must be returned by the man, who must move to the net and will generally be forced to lift the shuttle again. Thus, the smasher who has patience can work the attack with drops and smashes until the defenders are forced to hit a poor return and then smash for a winner.

A second weakness of this defensive position occurs when the attacking clear is hit over the woman's head. Since the man must be positioned to return the straight ahead drop or smash, the attacking clear directed toward the opposite side of the court will usually force a weak return.

The general mixed doubles play pattern consists of shots directed down the sidelines (drops, drives) and hard or half-court drives hit cross-court. This is identical to the "cat and mouse" play at the beginning of all doubles matches. The front court player must try to get into the line of flight of the shuttle in order to disrupt this half-court and drive pattern and force the opponents to lift the shuttle.

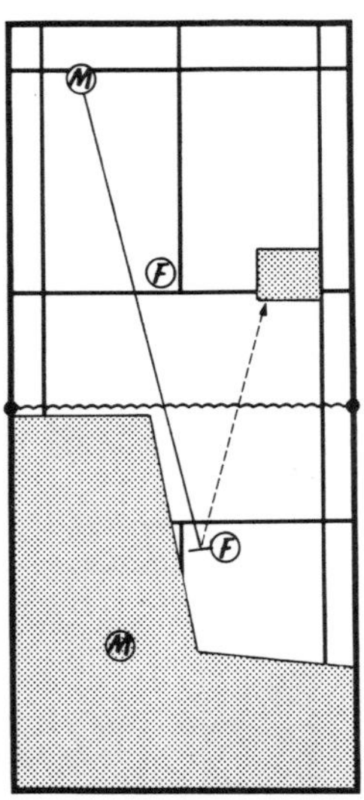

Figure 48

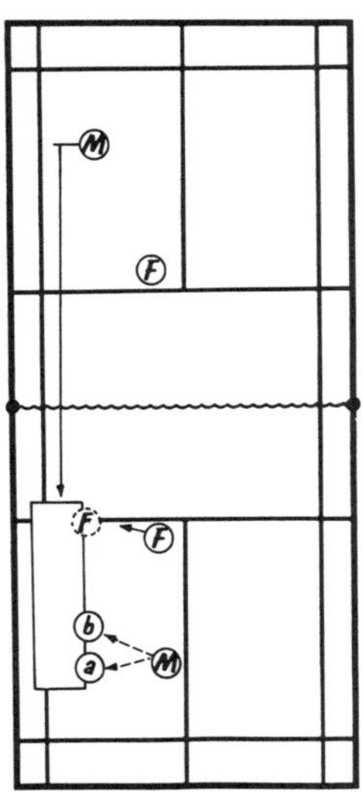

Figure 49

A good pattern to follow is to have the woman (front court player) stay on the same side of the court as the shuttle unless defending for the smash. Using this formation, shots hit straight ahead must be hit quicker and harder to prevent the woman from intercepting the shot and blocking it down the sideline for a winner. This harder-hit shuttle will carry deeper in the court and allow her partner to return the shuttle from a higher position above the floor, Figure 49-a.

The choice of shots hit above waist level is much better than those in which the man is forced to move forward and to the side and catch the shuttle below the knees (Figure 49-b). Interception of a high drive with deceptive straight-ahead and cross-court drives and drops place the opponents in a predicament of deciding which side of the court to defend (Figure 50). Thus, the female's strategic movement and anticipation (F in Figure 49) sets up her partner to control the rally. The female must be ready at all times to block a drive and move to smash the return for a winner.

Service and Receiver Positions

In order to begin the rally in the desired up and back formation, the male will serve from deeper in the court than in doubles (six feet behind the short service line) with the female positioning herself on the short service line (Figure 51). When serving from the odd (left) court, the female may wish to stand in front of her partner near the "T" so as not to restrict her partner's ability to serve wide (Figure 52). The receiving team will position themselves just as in regular doubles when the woman is receiving the service (Figure 51).

When the man is receiving the service, the woman has the option of (1) playing in the regular doubles formation, (2) moving up to mid-center court to help her partner with some drive returns or (3) play front

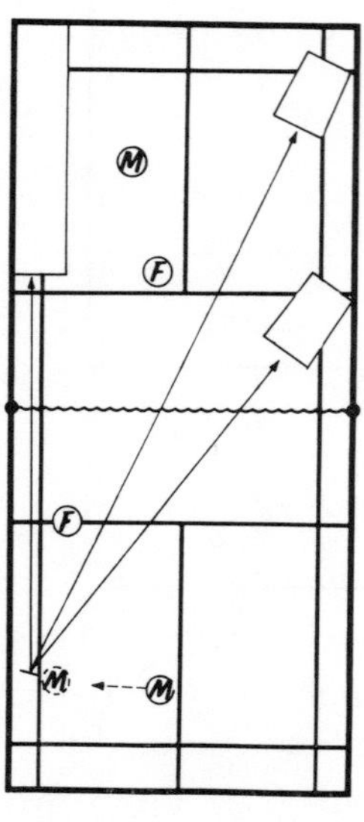

Figure 50

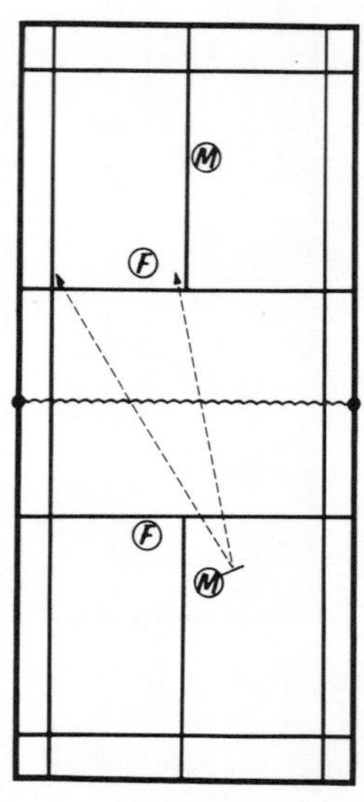

Figure 51

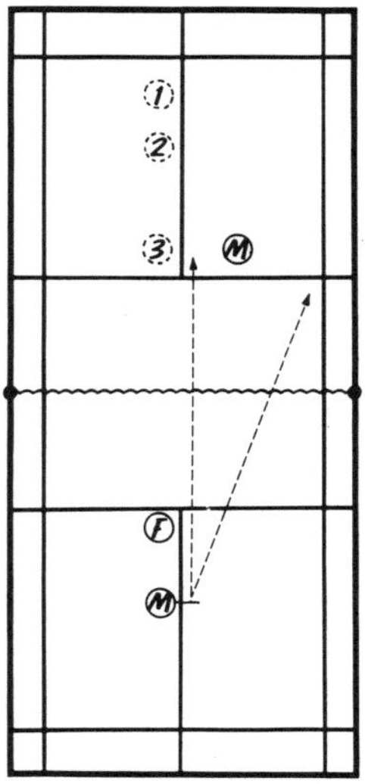

Figure 52

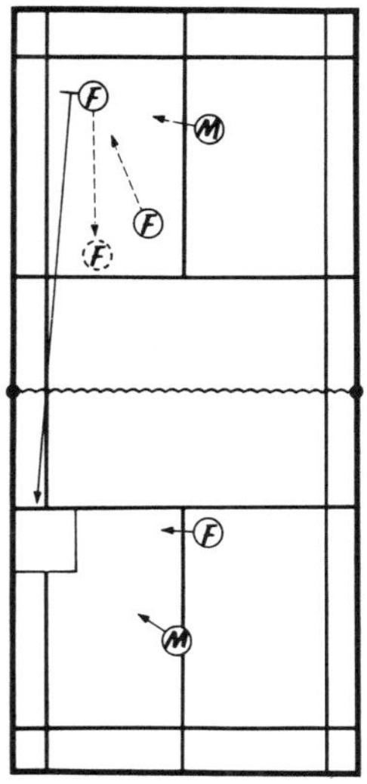

Figure 53

court, thus starting out in the attacking formation (Figure 52). In the latter position the male must rush the service very hard to force a weak return which will give him time to move back to control the backcourt.

In an effort to disrupt the formation with the woman in the front court, the server will often serve flick and drive serves to put her in the backcourt for the first shot. To counter this service strategy, the woman must try to hit an off-speed, steeply angled smash straight ahead (Figure 53) and follow the return into the front court position.

If she is able to anticipate the service and hit a hard smash, it could be directed down the side or down the center of the court as in doubles, and play the typical attacking position in hopes the man can cut off the return and hit a winning smash. Drop shot service returns are very risky in mixed doubles when the woman starts out in the forecourt position, as this shot is her only responsibility when her partner is serving.

CONDITIONING AND TRAINING PROGRAMS

When badminton is being contested between novice, intermediate, advanced or champion players, and the players are of equal skill, fitness becomes an important factor in determining the winner. A badminton player must be able to endure from 30 to 90 minutes of play during which 30-45% of the total time on court is active competition of play patterns characterized by abrupt changes in direction, explosive jumping, twisting and lunging, and stroking the shuttle with powerful full-arm hitting patterns from many body positions. Most rallies are from 4-10 seconds in duration with an average of 8 seconds between rallies. Badminton is probably the fastest racket sport, with a shot being hit about every .95 seconds in singles and every .85 seconds in doubles. Strength is a major factor in badminton, even though the racket and shuttle are lighter than the rackets and balls of other racket sports. A hard smash can leave the racket at speeds of 175-210 mph, and many clears, smashes and drives are struck with near-maximum effort, especially on the backhand.

Being in excellent physical condition provides a state of mental confidence for the player. He will feel comfortable and not hesitate to play in long, scrambling rallies and will be strong in the final game of a three game match.

The demands of playing badminton dictate that physical training programs must concentrate on the development of Speed, Strength, and Stamina, the three S's of badminton fitness. The task is to devise a physical fitness program incorporating the major physiological principles of conditioning into drills and play behaviors which will also increase badminton playing skills.

Two important physiological considerations applicable to badminton training programs are the following: (1) Law of Specificity — Badminton training patterns must simulate actual play behavior patterns as closely as possible, especially movement patterns at the intensity and duration of a competitive game and (2) Overload Principle — To increase fitness, training work levels must be greater than those to which the body is accustomed in badminton play. This applies primarily to strength, speed and stamina.

The following fitness training programs for badminton are based upon both the demands of the game and the related physiological principles. Three general categories of fitness programs will be described: (1) court play drills or pressure training, (2) shadow drills (on or off the court) and (3) traditional fitness training — interval training, strength training and calisthenics/stretching (flexibility).

Court Play Drills (Pressure Training)

There should be three basic variations in court play drills for badminton conditioning.

1. Ten seconds of high-intensity movement and stroking precede 10 seconds of light-work recovery. These 10-second work and rest hours should be repeated eight-to-ten times in succession. Simple routines should be developed in which a winning shot is hit after about 10 seconds. For example, player A (worker) hits all net drops while player B (setter) serves a high, deep singles serve and then hits alternating clears and drops, thus making player A move as far and fast as possible to reach the shuttle (shaded areas, Figure 54). After about five trips to the net, player A will smash the next clear and keep attacking with smashes until hitting a winner. Players A and B will then alternate as worker and setter after each rally. Any number of drills such as this can be developed, depending upon the skill of the players and the particular shots desired for practice. Players should work near maximum intensity for these short-duration drills and each rally should end with a winning shot. This drill simulates the typical play period for badminton with both a time and intensity overload.

2. During badminton one often gets in several long rallies which require a great deal of explosive movement and scrambling in order to retrieve the shuttle. During and after these rallies players often experience pain and local fatigue which is probably related to increased

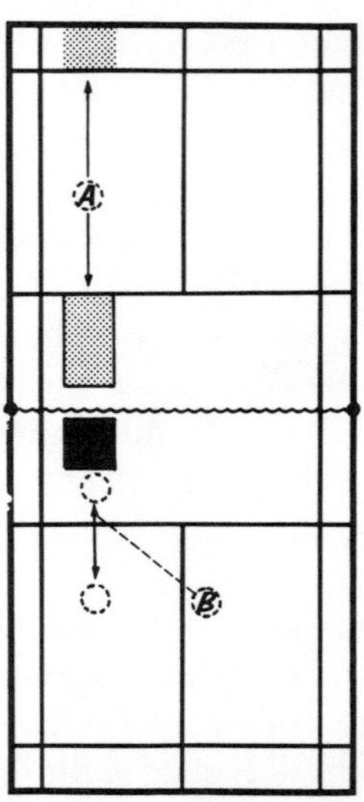

Figure 54

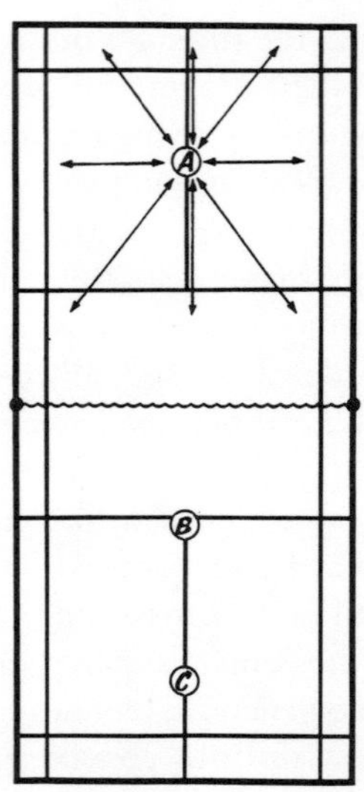

Figure 55

lactic acid production. Three player drills are excellent to prepare the player for these grueling rallies in competition. The general play is to have 30-second work bouts with 60-second low-intensity recovery periods. For example, player A (worker) on one side of the court alternates between hitting clears and drops. Player B (setter) plays the forecourt and player C (setter) plays the backcourt. Players B and C can hit the shuttle to any spot on the court (Figure 55) which makes player A work very hard to retrieve it. After about 30 seconds of play, player A will hit a winning smash down one of the sidelines. After each 30-second rally, the players rotate positions until each has had 30 seconds of intense work followed by a winning shot and 60 seconds of recovery. This routine should be repeated six to eight times in succession. Drills of this type require greater player skill than 10-second drills. Only the imagination of the coach and ability levels of players limit the variety of strokes that can be practiced during these drills. As in all badminton drills, the setters are very important as they must keep the rally continuous by introducing a new shuttle if one goes out of play and make the worker move to retrieve the shuttle at peak intensity.

3. The third type pattern should be the final series for the practice session. For this drill, player A (worker) must hit every shuttle to a given target area of the court (Figure 56). Player B (setter) will stay in this area and play shots to all areas of the court to make player A move at about 85 to 95 percent of maximum play intensity. The play will be continuous for one minute. If a shuttle is missed, the setter will introduce a new shuttle to provide continuous play. After a 90-second recovery period (any low-intensity activity), player A will repeat the same procedures, hitting to a new target area (1, 2, 3, or 4 of Figure 56). This series should be repeated three to four times in succession. As fitness increases, the work period should be lengthened in 15-second increments

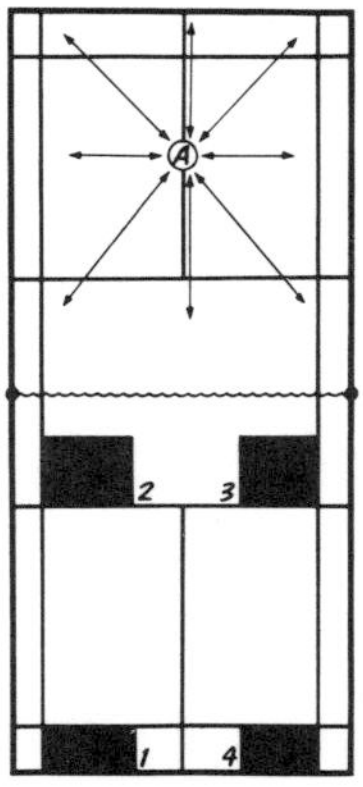

Figure 56

with the 90-second recovery period being held constant. Any player who can maintain four repetitions of this drill with three-minute continuous play periods is in excellent physical condition for playing badminton.

All three varieties of pressure training court play drills require high-intensity work bouts with low-intensity recovery period, a setter to pace the play and movement patterns to simulate the competitive game. The important work-recovery intervals for these drills should be followed for best results.

Shadow Drills (On or Off the Court)

While good for physical conditioning, shadow drills obviously lack the stroking skills required during a game. It is recommended that the same periods of work and recovery be employed as in the court play drills: 10 seconds work, 10 seconds recovery; 30 seconds work, 60 seconds recovery; and more than 60 seconds work, 90 seconds recovery.

The play of the shadow drills is to have one person move about the badminton court (or area of similar size) at an intensity similar to a competitive game. A partner may direct the player to various court areas by hand or arm signals.

Traditional Fitness Training

Windsprints and running. The same time intervals discussed in the shadow drill and court play drills should be used, with periods of maximum intensity. For example: 10 seconds work, 10 seconds rest; 30 seconds work, 60 seconds rest; and 60 or more seconds work, 90 seconds rest. The number of repetitions should be eight to ten; six to eight; and three to four, respectively. Although windsprint repetitions are less specific to badminton than the court play drills and shadow drills, they have the advantage of providing more consistent and greater intensity overloads. Coaches and players having limited court time will find these drills very effective for fitness conditioning.

Rope skipping. This excellent endurance training method is probably next best to playing a series of badminton games. Players should work up to 45 minutes of continuous rope skipping at a rate of 80 to 120 jumps per minute. Players under 25 years of age should skip at heart rates between 165 and 185 beats per minute. Skipping rate can be increased or decreased to stabilize the heart rate in this training range.

Strength training. There are probably more jumps, lunges, and full hard strokes in badminton play than in any other racket sport. Unfortunately, research has not established the minimum or maximum strength levels desired for badminton players. Muscular strength and endurance of the arm can be improved by standing about six feet from a wall and hitting a shuttle against the wall several times in succession. Build up to 100 successive hits of a given stroke. Badminton players should include exercises for strengthening wrist flexion, forearm supination and pronation, arm extension, leg flexion and extension, and plantar flexion and extension. Weight training for badminton should begin with weights that can be raised rapidly 10 times. When the weight can be rapidly raised 15 times during the arm exercises and 20 times during the leg exercises, the next heavier weight should be used. As standard practice, two to three sets of each exercise should be completed during the workout.

Flexibility. Calisthenics and stretching exercises should precede each workout or competition. A program of 5 to 15 minutes should be developed with special emphasis placed on the ankle, achilles, hamstrings and shoulder for the badminton player. Static stretching following an intense workout may help to reduce muscle soreness.

Many people erroneously believe distance running to be ideal training for badminton. Both the tempo of the run and the foot strike patterns are different. Swimming, like distance running, increases endurance but, like running, it does not train patterns of movement comparable to those required for competitive badminton. The best fitness training programs for badminton simulate the competitive game movement patterns and overload the work intensity and duration through repetitive bouts of intense exercise and recovery (pressure training).

Playing with wrist or ankle weights or a very heavy racket do not seem to be effective training methods for badminton as skill levels seem to be inhibited and physical training is not increased as much as by other methods.

Warm-Up for Badminton Competition

Warm-up for badminton consists of (1) preparing oneself physiologically for activity requiring strength, speed and stamina and (2) executing several shots to become accustomed to the court area and playing conditions.

Physiological preparation should include active exertion, i.e., running in place, to work up a slight sweat. Stretching exercises should also be done to prevent cramps and other injuries and muscle soreness (after playing). The player should be physiologically ready to play before entering the court for the match.

The skill warm-up is often limited to 5 minutes of hitting shots on the court before the match begins. Most players should hit clears, drives, drops and then smashes. End the warm-up with some easy stroking and taking some serves. The warm-up is not a practice session.

In doubles, warm up with your own partner and develop a routine to execute the shots you want to hit before the game starts.

When warming up with your opponent, as in singles, don't show your opponent all of your shots. Let him see them for the first time during the match.

TEACHING AIDS

It is important for teachers to continually ask themselves how much can be learned by the students in a given time. Additionally, one has to evaluate from this as to what portion of that time is available to the individual learner. If one is giving instruction to a group, this "time" to the student is considered equal to all. However, as the teacher observing the class, it is readily seen that the attention from every student is different. This behavior is one of the most difficult assessments the teacher has to make. It is at this point the teacher starts assessing what is the most effective procedure to adopt in order to assure the most effective learning environment. From this point the teacher may apply the various techniques and methods of teaching. The effectiveness relates not only to these techniques and methods, but also to the personality of the teacher. As we all know, none of us can be Bob Hope just because we have his jokes.

Assuming all teachers have the same materials to teach a sport as badminton, it does not guarantee that the student will learn this material. Thus, the teaching hints given to this chapter may or may not in total apply to you as the teacher.

Basic motor learning theories that apply to learning any skill such as badminton are the following:

1. Thinking through a movement facilitates the learning of complex motor skills.
2. Practicing basic techniques aids the development of the skill.
3. Kinesthetic perception (a feeling of space) is used to learn a skill.
4. The time to practice a skill is relative to the attention span of the learner and endurance (over-practice may diminish skillful performance).

One of the most important decisions the teacher has to make in teaching any skill is to develop objectives that are realistic and that can be achieved by most students. In teaching beginning badminton one cannot expect the student to learn to play badminton at a high skill level in one semester or grading period. However, one could expect a relatively high level of skill in some segments of the game. In determining these segments as a true objective to be learned, success may not be realized because of differing student interest and motivation. At this point the teacher may assess concomitant learning within the scope of learning to play badminton. As an example, in beginning badminton a realistic objective is to learn to serve a high, deep and low, short serve. Needless to say, if the teacher spends a complete semester or grading period on these two objectives, student interest and motivation would be lost in a few lessons. Thus the teacher must create a pattern of instruction that allows the student to play the game as soon as possible, even though the level of skill may be very poor. The teacher can capitalize on this by keeping students interested and motivated. At the same time, employing the techniques of teaching the serves which are the primary objectives can be learned at a fairly high level. Also, by having students play they will better understand how ineffectively they are serving, giving the teacher an opportunity to stress the main objectives throughout the semester or grading period.

In teaching beginning badminton, the teacher should present to the student the objectives of the course, keeping in mind that these objectives can be learned and also measured. As in most sports, the sequence for learning badminton is also important to skill development. The sequence for teaching beginning badminton is outlined later in this chapter.

Competitive Drills and Modified Games

Many times the introduction of competition into a practice or drill session does much to stimulate the interest of students. Many of the developmental drills included in this report are easily adaptable to the competitive aspect. In addition to any of those so chosen, the following are recommended as having been successfully used.

Doubles-Doubles

This is an original game developed by a teacher for use in large badminton classes. It can be played by beginners or those with more experience and can be equally exciting to both groups. It is particularly recommended for beginners. It should not, however, be used to the exclusion of a regular doubles game. It should be played according to official rules for doubles **except** that there are four people on each side of the net instead of two. Two people on each side are allowed to serve, after the first service, as in an official game. When the side is out, the two people on the back half of the court on the side which is just coming in to serve step forward to become the servers. They then serve until the side is out. Then the back court players on the other side step forward to exchange places with the forecourt players, thus becoming servers, etc.

It is important in this system that the player in the back court, behind the receiver of serve, steps back far enough to allow the receiver space to make an adequate return. The two playing the forecourt should be warned not to back up too far to make a return. The players in the back court are able to watch the front players and avoid colliding with them.

Half-Court Singles

The center line may be extended to the net temporarily with tape. This game can also be played by using the team concept, having five players on a team. Like baseball, the team provides the teacher with an order of play (batting order). The game is played by official singles rules, except no one player is allowed to score more than three points. This does not allow one person on the team to dominate the game. Substitutions are made each time a team member loses a rally. By using the team concept, the teacher could have twenty students playing singles, utilizing only one court. This game generates team spirit and allows the teacher time to talk to groups of students about strategy, stroking, etc., during the rallies.

Teaching Expressions

High, Deep Serve

1. Keep the feet on the floor until the shuttle is contacted.
2. Think out as well as up when hitting the serve.
3. Follow through high in a vertical plane over your left shoulder.
4. Always cock the wrist before the serve (remember, cocking means hyperextension of the wrist) and supination of the forearm (clockwise rotation of right forearm).
5. Uncock the wrist with force at point of contact.
6. Aim for the back boundary line.
7. Extend the arm in the follow-through.
8. Avoid rushing the stroke.
9. Take comfortable stance and shift weight from the back to front foot during the swing.
10. Drop shuttle, don't throw it at the racket. Open the hand and let it drop from about shoulder height.

Low, Short Serve

1. Start serve in a cocked position, arm back in hitting position.
2. Hit through the shuttle.
3. Keep racket head below the hand at contact.
4. Keep both feet stationary until contact.
5. Shift weight from back to front foot (except for the backhand short serve).
6. Hit all serves with the same preparation.
7. Learn the long doubles serve and use it intelligently.
8. Stand approximately three feet behind the short service line near the center line (except for the backhand serve).

9. Hold shuttle at the base between the thumb and index finger, drop the shuttle and swing the racket slowly through the shuttle.
10. Follow through to the net in a flat trajectory.
11. Contact shuttle in front of the body below waist level (see serving rules in Appendix).
12. Keep wrist firm, don't uncock during the swing.

Overhead Clear

1. Hit off rear foot for maximum power.
2. Hit shuttle higher than opponent's extended racket.
3. Inward rotation of the forearm on contact of racket and shuttle (outward rotation for backhand).
4. Always hit shuttle as soon as possible.
5. Meet the shuttle with a flat racket or surface without any cutting or slicing motion.
6. Hit shuttle up and out.
7. Aim for the back boundary line.
8. Contact shuttle with an extended arm.
9. Rotate body in making the swing.
10. There must be rapid acceleration of racket swing just prior to contact with shuttle.
11. Keep elbows away from the body during the stroke.

Overhead Drop

1. Think smash to create deception.
2. Use quick drop shot when opponent is out of position.
3. Use same motion as clear and smash.
4. Use loop drop when opponent is in good position.

Smash

1. Take the shuttle high (forehand).
2. Vary the speed of the smash.
3. Contact the shuttle in front of the body.

Drive

1. Reach for the shuttle.
2. Hit through the shuttle.
3. Keep racket in line of flight.
4. Use side-arm throwing motion.
5. Hit shuttle in line with lead foot.
6. Hit with flat face of racket.
7. Turn body sideways to the net.

Developmental Drills

1. **Mimetic drills**
   A. Practice throwing imaginary ball to simulate stroking action.
   B. Practice hitting imaginary shuttlecock to simulate executing different strokes, i.e., overhead clears (forehand and backhand), underhand clears (forehand and backhand). Listen for swishing sound at contact point of shuttle.
   C. Practice moving to various positions on the court from the "ready" position.
   D. Practice moving to court position and executing imaginary swing before returning to base position.

2. **Hitting shuttlecock or fleece ball against wall**
   A. Stand approximately five feet from wall.
   B. Specify time limit for hitting (2-3 minutes).
   C. Have student count number of hits during this period (can be competitive drill).

3. **Rope Skipping**
   A. Specify number of jumps.
   B. Set competition for number of jumps in a given time.
   C. Increase time for conditioning.

4. **Use of Weights**

   Use weights for forearm and wrist strength. Use a round stick about one foot long and attach weights of approximately five pounds to a four foot length of light rope. Have student hold stick with arms extended at shoulder level and roll the weight up and down as many times as desired.

5. **Partner Drills on the Court**

   Place four people on each side of the court. Two people stand in backcourt on each side to practice overhead clears with their partners in the opposing backcourt. Two people stand at net position on each side practicing net shots (hair-pin and cross-court). After a specified time players change positions.

6. **Short Service Drill**

   Lines may be marked or masking tape used on the walls for service practice. The line should be net height (5 feet), and another line placed 6-10 inches higher. Have the students stand same distance from the wall as one would from the net on the playing court (6½-10 feet). As skills increase, lower the line closer to the five foot line. This drill can be used for competition, noting the number of shots between the lines for a given number of attempts. . .

7. **Target Hitting**

   Hula-hoops or towels placed at various points on the court make good targets to practice accuracy in hitting drops and clears. This drill can also be competitive by having a point system for hitting the shuttle into the hoops. This exercise may be used for high, deep serve and low, short serve.

8. **Fleece Ball Drill**

   Fleece balls may be hung by a cord from a basketball goal (or other gymnasium equipment) at various heights for practice of various strokes (overhead, drives, etc.)

9. **Clock Drill**

   Students assume themselves to be the center of a clock. From this position the instructor will call out different numbers of the clock hour. Students practice their footwork to move to these various positions as well as practice an imaginary stroke upon getting to the number position. After executing the imaginary stroke, students go back to the center of the clock position (base or ready position). This drill may be used to develop strokes using various shots from positions on the clock.

10. **Bouncing Shuttle or Fleece Ball on the Racket**

    The objective is to gain control, contact shuttle or ball in center of racket, hit softly, alternating forehand and backhand position, learn cut shots and slices (making shuttle tumble), and learn to hit shuttle from the lunging position. Competition can be held by counting the number of hits in 30 seconds. Players should switch to shuttles after becoming competent with the fleece ball. Everyone in the class can practice this drill on one or two counts. The teacher should check for correct forehand and backhand grips, and the stroking motion for hitting each shuttle or fleece ball with the cocked wrist for both forehand and backhand shots.

11. **Team Net Play (King of the Court)**

    Several players can be on each team. Play begins by the first player hitting short service which is returned by a net shot by the receiver. Play continues with each player alternating **underhand** hits (similar to table tennis) until each player has hit the shuttle before beginning the second round. All shots must be played in front of the short service line, any place within the doubles side boundary lines. The purpose is to make the opponent run to return the shuttle. Each time an error is made, that person sits out until all players on a team have been eliminated. As the sides become smaller, a great deal of movement can be required. This is a good game for players of all skills and is fun during the first week of the beginning class.

Singles Drills

With players paired off on the court, several drills can be used to teach stroking and improve accuracy in stroking the basic shots. Some of these are:

1. One player hits all drops from near the baseline and the other player hits all underhand clears. Players alternate after a specified number of consecutive hits (10, 20, 50, etc.).
2. Both players play in the area of the baseline and hit clears. Any shuttle falling short of the long doubles service line or beyond the baseline will not be played. This method gives immediate feedback on whether the clears are of appropriate length.
3. Both players play underhand net drops. As skills increase, cross-courts and cut shots will be attempted. A short service and net game can be played and points scored as in a regular game. Shots falling beyond the short service line are not hit and are scored as faults.
4. **High, deep service practice:** Shuttle must land between long doubles service line and baseline (count number on target, 10 serves and rotate players). Some players place towels or objects in service areas as targets and count the number of hits.
5. **Service and service return game:** Server hits shuttle as in No. 4 above. If in target area, service returner hits straight ahead clear which will fall between baseline and long doubles service line to score a point. Drops or other returns can be included as well as clear returns.
6. Players can hit drives at each other. Use the following combinations: (a) both players hit straight ahead, (b) both hit cross-courts from each side of the body and (c) one player hits all straight ahead and the other all cross-courts.
7. One player plays near the T and hits drives into the body of the opponent. Opponent is playing one step in front of long doubles service line and returns with backhand defense whenever possible.

Basic Court Positions, Strokes Used and Available Shots

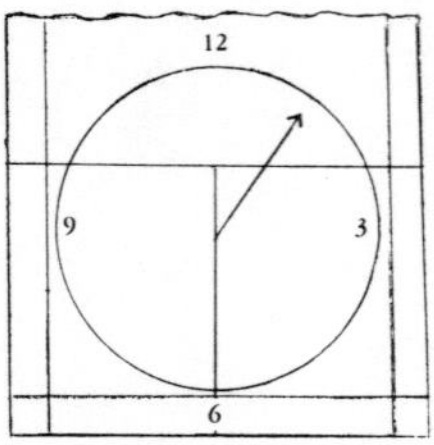

1 o'clock position

Stroke:
Underhand

Shots:
High Deep Clear
Straight Drop
Cross-Court Drop

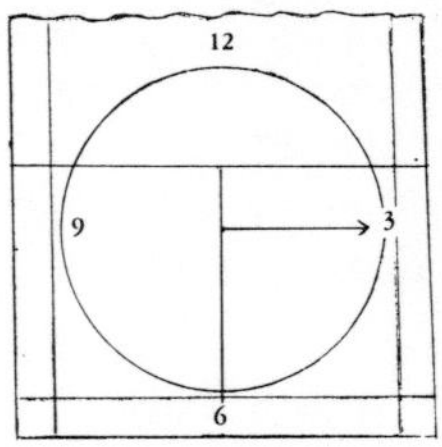

3 o'clock position

Stroke:
Sidearm

Shots:
Attacking Clear
Defensive Clear
1/2 Court Drive
Straight Drop
Cross-Court Drop

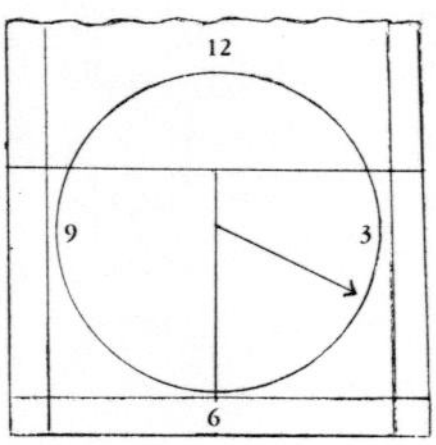

5 o'clock position

Stroke:
Overhead

Shots:
High Deep Clear
Attacking Clear
Straight Drop
Cross-Court Drop

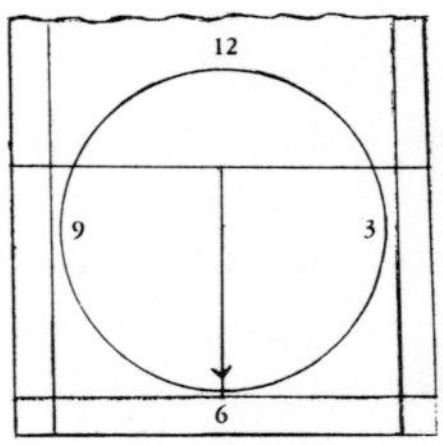

6 o'clock position

Stroke:
Overhead

Shots:
High Deep Clear
Attacking Clear
Straight Drop
Cross-Court Drop

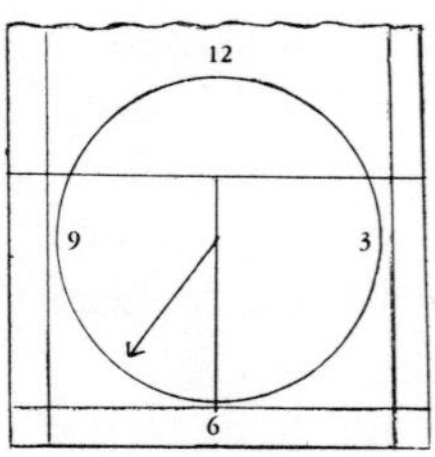

7 o'clock position (Backhand)

Stroke:
Overhead

Shots:
High Deep Clear
Attacking Clear
Straight Drop
Cross-Court Drop

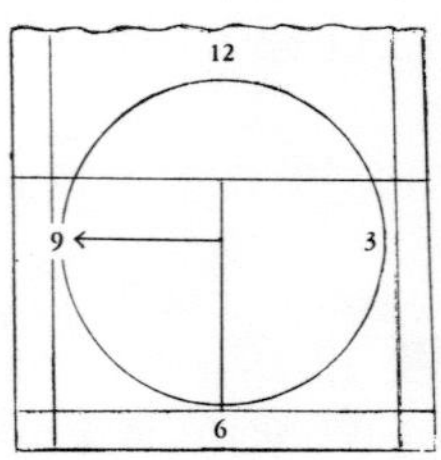

9 o'clock position (Backhand)

Stroke:
Sidearm

Shots:
Attacking Clear
Defensive Clear
1/2 Court Drive
Straight Drop
Cross Court Drop

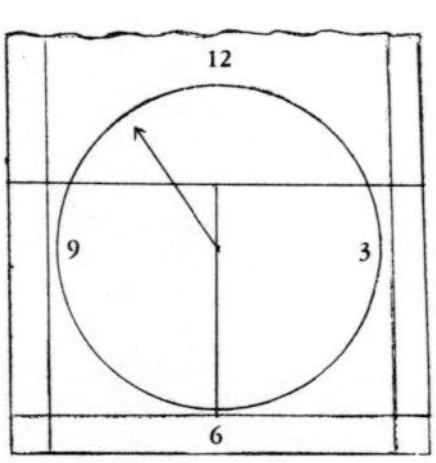

11 o'clock position (Backhand)

Stroke:
Underhand

Shots:
High Deep Clear
Straight Drop
Cross-Court Drop

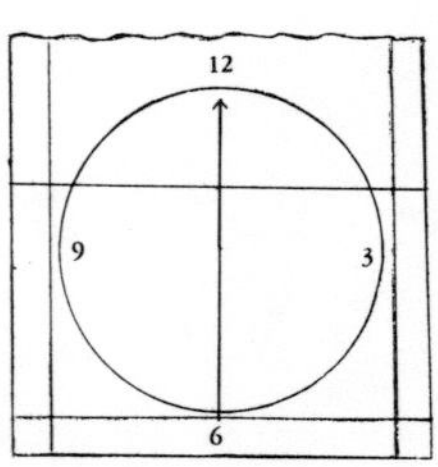

12 o'clock position (Backhand)

Stroke:
In-Front
Shots:
Block
Clear

LESSON PLANS
(With Motor Learning Concepts in Italics)

LESSON NO. 1

I. Introductory Session
  A. Facts about game
    Establishing a concept of purpose.
    1. Nature of the game
      a. Equipment
        1) Care
        2) Cost
        3) Selection
      b. Court
        1) Basic dimension
        2) Net height
    This lesson will give support to level I.
    Structuring the environment for supplementary feedback.
    2. Scoring
      a. Singles
      b. Doubles
      c. Laws for discussion
    Mental and verbal rehearsals.
    3. Demonstration
      a. Emphasis on a variety of shots
      b. Physical requirements
    Motivation-Arousal

II. Holding and Cocking
  A. Forehand
    Muscular strength, power endurance, and flexibility will be factors in learning this grip and cocked position.
    1. Grip and cocked position
      a. 8 students to a court with 4 on each side.
      b. A simulated drill without bird.
    Mental rehearsals.
  B. Backhand
    1. Grip and cocked position
    2. Simulated drill without bird.
    The internal information (kinesthetics) continues to be processed through the student and filtering should be great at this stage.
  C. Hammer grip
    1. Use simulated drill without bird.

D. Observe for incorrect grip during drill.
E. During demonstration, students form a semicircle.
Possibly clarify his/her knowledge, proficiency expectations are reinforced.
F. Students volley with partners.
Motivational

LESSON NO. II

Equipment: Rackets, fleece balls, skipping ropes, 4 nets, shuttlecocks, record charts for scoring at each station.

I. Introduction of Stations
This lesson takes the student into the many levels of his ability (Level II) and the sensory input toward the motor output. Visualspatial orientation, depth perception sense and visual perception speed, kinesthetic sense and the muscular abilities will be given sensory input.
A. Count station
1. ½ class will work on clear shots
2. Stress holding and cocking
B. Rope skipping (8 students)
1. Practice
2. Record number of consecutive jumps
Training for motor response.
Feedback
C. Fleece ball (8 students)
1. Practice hitting fleece ball against the wall standing 3 feet from wall hitting underhanded.
Skill specifics
2. Record score for 1 minute of hitting.
Feedback
D. Use part of class time for play
Motivational

LESSON NO. III

Equipment: Rackets, skip ropes, weight training equipment.

I. Low Short Serve
A. Legal Serve
Regulatory cues

B. Starting position
C. Holding and dropping
Training for motor response
D. Straighten arm, wrist cocked
E. Rotate body
Directing attention
F. Remain cocked up on contact
G. Follow thru

II. Use part of class time for play
Motivational

III. Half-court singles
Feedback

IV. Stations
A. Rope Skip
B. Weight training
Feedback

LESSON NO. IV

1. High Deep Serve (Hit to singles court)
Directing attention to a specific skill which has regulatory cues and feedback characteristics.
A. Racket position for legal serve
B. Starting position (center of court)
C. Holding and dropping shuttlecock in front of body
D. Straighten arm — wrist cocked
E. Rotate body (shift weight)
F. Unlock wrist — upon contact with shuttlecock

G. Follow thru (vertical plane)

II. Half-court singles (½ class)
Decisions must be made on the basis of the receivers positioning. Cognitive awareness and the choice or decision from the long term store is the process of learning in the half-court singles.

III. Serve-drill — (½ class)
A. Serve deep go to end of line.
B. Rotate class to half-court singles, to serve drill, to stations (fleece ball, rope skip, weight training).
1. Record where appropriate.

LESSON NO. V

Equipment: Rackets, shuttlecocks

I. Low Short Serve (½ class)

These skills give double duty to the game of badminton. The verbal points of emphasis reinforce the value of the learning of them correctly and quickly.

  A. Serve short, go to end of line
  B. Make corrections

II. High Deep Serve (½ class)

  A. Serve deep, go to end of line
  B. Make corrections

III. Evaluate for future references, grouping, seeding, etc.

Mental and verbal rehearsals

IV. Play half-court singles

V. Demonstrate doubles play

  A. Positions

  Problem-solving

  B. Scoring

  Short-term store

LESSON NO. VI

I. Introduces the following stations

This is an area of learning which reinforces the filtration of learning into the limited capacity channel.

  A. Basketball net
    1. Forehand
    2. Backhand
  B. Wall drill on mat
    1. Forehand
    2. Backhand
  C. Towel (backhand)
  D. Serve between rope and net

II. Game to develop clear

Rehearsal and internal information

  A. Hit first over net
  B. Use length of floor

III. Doubles-Doubles

LESSON NO. VII

I. Footwork
   A. Ready position
   B. Movement patterns from center of gravity
      Structuring the pattern or plan as in the clock method.
   C. Clock positions
      1. 1 o'clock (forehand)
      2. 3 o'clock (forehand)
      3. 5 o'clock (forehand)
      4. 6 o'clock (forehand
      5. 7 o'clock (backhand)
      6. 9 o'clock (backhand)
      7. 11 o'clock (backhand)
      Gives the student an excellent chance to use the whole part of the skill and provides a pattern for retention, mental and verbal rehearsal.
   D. Use all clock positions with additional steps.
   E. Return from all clock positions to ready position
II. Doubles-Doubles
   A. Emphasis footwork
   B. Competition
   C. Scoring

LESSON NO. VIII

I. Forehand Overhead
      Differential relaxation becomes more important at this point. The student is made aware of this while trying to hit clear shots with sufficient distance.
   A. Defensive clear
   B. Attacking clear
II. Backhand Overhead
   A. Defensive clear
   B. Attacking clear
III. Wall drill on mat
      Rehearsal
   A. Forehand
   B. Backhand
   C. Make corrections
IV. Doubles-Doubles
      Long term store and memory loop. Choice delay.

LESSON NO. IX

I. Forehand Overhead

Short term store and filter processes.

- A. Fast Drop
- B. Loop Drop
- C. Smash

II. Backhand Overhead

- A. Fast Drop
- B. Loop Drop
- C. Smash

III. Stress feel on drops

Differential relaxation

IV. Drill with ½ court singles

- A. Drop shot-clear shot

V. Team Badminton

LESSON NO. X

I. Forehand Underhand

A new skill involving Level II and III.

- A. Defensive clear
- B. Net shots
  1. Straight ahead
  2. Cross-court

II. Backhand Underhand

Differential relaxation abilities in the Level II of Motor Skill Learning are involved.

- A. Defensive clear
- B. Net shots
  1. Straight ahead
  2. Cross-court
  3. Straight ahead

III. Drill on underhand shots

The drills under III are new and have built-in corrections.

- A. Underhand to underhand hit
- B. Straight across
- C. Cross-court to cross-court
- D. Straight across to cross-court

IV. Use of stations as needed for special problems and practice (Basketball net drill for those needing smash drill)

LESSON NO. XI

I. Forehand drive
   A. Changing speed (deep-half court)
   B. Cross-court
   C. Straight ahead
II. Backhand drive
   A. Changing speed (deep-half court)
   B. Cross-court
   C. Straight ahead
III. Doubles-Doubles

Again relying upon this drill to place into the long-term store, scoring, strategy, usage of special shots.

LESSON NO. XII

I. Testing

Rehearsal loop, filter limited capacity, choice delay and finally the output with continuing internal information being processed.

   A. High Deep Serve
      1. Record
      2. Assign teams to court for testing

II.
   A. Doubles play on remaining courts
   B. Challengers for doubles play will work at stations until turn at court doubles play.

LESSON NO. XIII

I. Testing
   A. Low short serve
      1. Record
II. Team Singles on available courts

Spatial-temporal pattern.

LESSON NO. XIV

I. Basic strategy
   Short term store
   A. Singles
   B. Doubles
II. Pre-arranged singles tournament
   A. Better players handicapped (Serve testing can be basis for handicaps)
   B. Play round-robin by courts.

LESSON NO. XV

I. Follow-up tournament
II. Provide stations with final recording for
   A. Fleece ball
   B. Rope skip
   C. Weight training

LESSON NO. XVI

I. Service test
   A. High deep service
   B. Low short service
II. Written exam

Grading Points (use grade scale)

1.	High deep serve —	35
2.	Low short serve —	35
3.	Written exam —	20
4.	Wall volley (fleece ball) —	10
		100

Evaluation

Skill Tests

The following skill tests may be utilized for measurement and evaluation:

1. High clear — mark a regulation badminton court as follows:

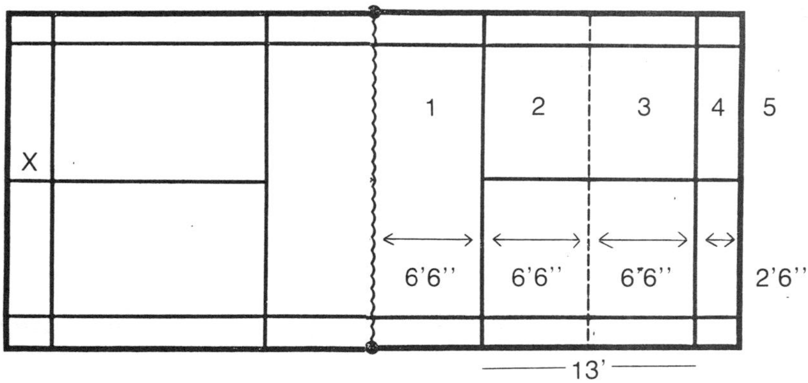

Administration of the Test

The subject stands between the base line and the long doubles restraining line as indicated by the "X" in the diagram. From this position, both the forehand and backhand clear test are taken.

1. *Forehand clear test:* The subject stands in correct position for the forehand clear at the spot indicated in the diagram. From this position, he places the shuttlecock on the *forehand face* of the racket, tosses the shuttlecock overhead, and strokes a *forehand clear* as far as possible.
2. *Backhand clear test:* The subject stands in correct position for the backhand clear at the spot indicated in the diagram. From this position, he places the shuttlecock on the *forehand face* of the racket, tosses the shuttlecock overhead, and strokes a *backhand clear* as far as possible.

Scoring: Each subject is given seven trials on the forehand and seven on the backhand. The best five of these seven trials is the subject's score. As indicated in the diagram, the deeper the clear is hit, the higher the score. To be scored, a shuttlecock must fall within the sidelines of the doubles court or the sidelines extended. A shuttlecock falling on a restraining line is given the higher value of the line in question.

2. Wall Volley Test[1]

[1]Miller, F.A., *Research Quarterly*, 22:2, May 1951, p. 211.

Administration of the Test

Equipment	1.	Badminton racket in good condition
	2.	New outdoor shuttlecock (sponge-end)
	3.	Accurate stop watch
	4.	Score cards and pencils
Markings	1.	Wall — a 1'' line extended across the wall 7'6'' from the floor and parallel to it. The wall space should be at least 10' wide and preferably 15' or more high.
	2.	Floor — a straight line 10' from the wall extended the length of the wall distance and parallel to the wall.
Assistants Needed	1.	Timer (gives signal, ''ready, go'' and ''stop'')
	2.	Scorer (counts the number of legal hits)
	3.	Recorder (makes a record of good hits)

The subject should be given the opportunity to *practice* for one minute before the first trial is given. If there is ample wall space, several players can practice at the same time and also can be tested at the same time, as there is a 10' distance between players. A short *rest period* of at least 30 seconds should be allowed between trials. Practice should not be allowed between trials.

On the signal, ''ready, go,'' the subject serves the shuttlecock in a legal manner against the wall from behind the 10' floor line. The serve puts the shuttlecock in a position to be rallied with a clear on each rebound. If the serve hits on or above the 7'6'' wall line, that hit counts as one point and each following rebound hit made on or above the 7'6'' wall line when the subject is behind the 10' floor line counts as one point. The hit is not counted if any part of the foot goes over the 10'restraining line. (Due to the fact that a subject encounters difficulty when trying to look at the line on the floor along with watching the shuttlecock, it is suggested that a chalk line 3'' back from the 10' line be added, and the subject told to stay behind that line if possible. This allows the foot to slide as much as 3'' without penalizing the person being tested. Also, the scorer should say ''back'' whenever the subject consistently goes over the line). The hit is not counted if the shuttlecock goes below the 7'6'' wall line. However, either in the case of the foot going over the 10' line or the shuttlecock hitting below the 7'6'' line, the subject is permitted to keep the shuttlecock in play. The shuttlecock may be stopped at any time and re-started with a legal service from behind the 10' floor line. If the shuttlecock is missed and falls to the floor, the subject picks up the same shuttlecock as quickly as possible, gets behind the 10'floor line, and puts the shuttlecock into play with a legal service.

An accumulative number of hits made within 30 seconds is given to the recorder by the scorer for each individual. When the timer gives the signal ''stop'' a total number of hits is given to the recorder. Three 30-second trials are given. Any stroke may be used to keep the shuttlecock in play. A ''carried bird'' or a double hit is counted as good if the hit eventually goes on or above the 7'6'' wall line. The subject may step in front of the 10' line in order to keep the shuttlecock in play, but hits failing to follow the specifications given above do not count. The sponge-end shuttlecock will bounce if the shuttlecock falls to the floor. The subject does not have to pick up the shuttlecock if he can keep the shuttlecock in play in any manner. The score consists of the sum of three trials.

3. Deep Service Test — mark a regulation badminton court as follows:

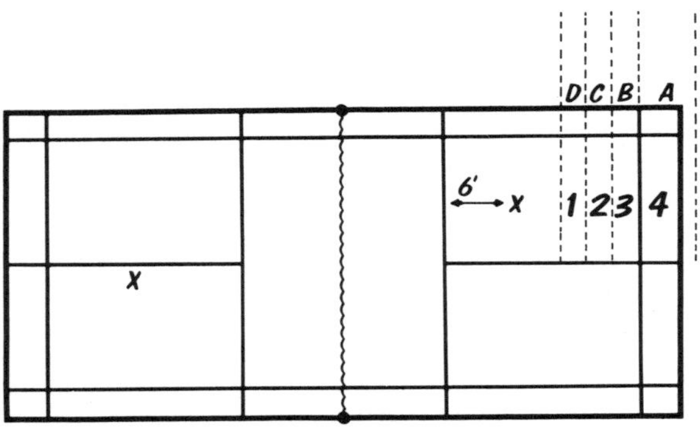

— this line is 2'' behind end line.

Administration of the Test

Equipment 1. Ten nylon shuttlecocks (medium speed)
2. Score cards and pencils
3. Two badminton rackets

Markings 1. Use plastic tape 1½'' wide for marking court
2. Distances include the width of the tape

The server is given twenty warm-up serves. Then the next ten consecutive serves are scored. The receiver stands holding his racket over his head with his arm extended. Any shuttle the receiver can cut off without moving is an ''F'' and is scored as zero. Any fault serve is an ''F'' and is scored zero. The total possible score is 40 points. Each area has a point value of 1 to 4: D = 1 point, C = 2 points, B = 3 points, and A = 4 points. The serve must be high and deep to avoid having it cut off by the receiver.

Knowledge Tests

Knowledge or written tests should be given over assigned material as a part of the educational process.

GRADE SCALE

A+		1	2	5	A+	10	15	20	25	A+	50
A	92.5-100	.96	1.9	4.81	A	9.62	14.43	19.24	24.05	A	48.10
A-		.93	1.85	4.63	A-	9.26	13.89	18.52	23.15	A-	46.30
B	85.0-92.4	.89	1.78	4.44	B	8.88	13.32	17.76	22.20	B	44.40
B-		.85	1.70	4.25	B-	8.50	12.75	17.00	21.25	B-	42.50
C	77.5-84.9	.81	1.63	4.06	C	8.12	12.18	16.24	20.30	C	40.60
C-		.78	1.55	3.88	C-	7.76	11.64	15.52	19.40	C-	38.80
D	70.0-77.49	.74	1.48	3.69	D	7.38	11.07	14.76	18.45	D	36.90
D-		.70	1.40	3.50	D-	7.00	10.50	14.00	17.30	D-	35.00
F	69.99 or below	.66	1.33	3.31	F	6.62	9.93	13.24	16.55	F	33.10
F-		0	0	0	F-	0	0	0	0	F-	0

APPENDIX

Appendix

A. Rules and Etiquette Interpretations

There are several factors that can make badminton or any sport more enjoyable to play. Each sport has its own customs and mannerisms. Badminton is no exception. In many tournaments, the players will keep score and play up through the quarterfinals without having a referee.

Below is a list of factors which should be included in badminton etiquette:

1. Know the rules well.
2. Keep score and call it out periodically.
3. If you tie an opponent at one of the setting points, 13 or 14-all in all games (except for ladies singles, which is 9 or 10-all), ask your opponent if he/she wishes to set the game.
4. Make sure your serve is legal (no feints, racket head in proper position and below the waist).
5. If the shuttle falls on your side of the court and your opponent has won the rally, return the shuttle to your opponent immediately; don't just leave it near the net or shove it into the other court. Hit it directly to your opponent.
6. Line calls can often cause a dispute. It is your responsibility to call the lines on your side of the court, not your opponent's. If there are no linesmen, which is generally the case except for the finals of tournaments, and you are unable to see the shuttle land, you might ask your opponent if the shuttle was good. If neither player sees the shuttle land, play a let. If you have a good view of the shuttle and are unable to determine whether it is in or out, the shuttle should be played as good. Remember, if the cork (base) hits inside or on the line, the shuttle is good, or "in." Try to call lines quickly, firmly, and accurately.
7. Play is continuous in badminton. Try to be in the proper court to serve or return service.
8. If you warm up with your opponent, work together to give each other a chance to hit the shots each of you desire. Remember, warm-up is not practice.
9. Do not play indifferently against an inferior opponent.

THE LAWS OF BADMINTON

Court

1. (a) The court shall be laid out as in the following Diagram "A" (except in the case provided for in paragraph (b) of this Law) and to the measurements there shown, and shall be defined preferably by white or yellow lines, or, if this is not possible, by other easily distinguishable lines, 40 mm. (1-1/2 inches) wide.

BADMINTON COURT

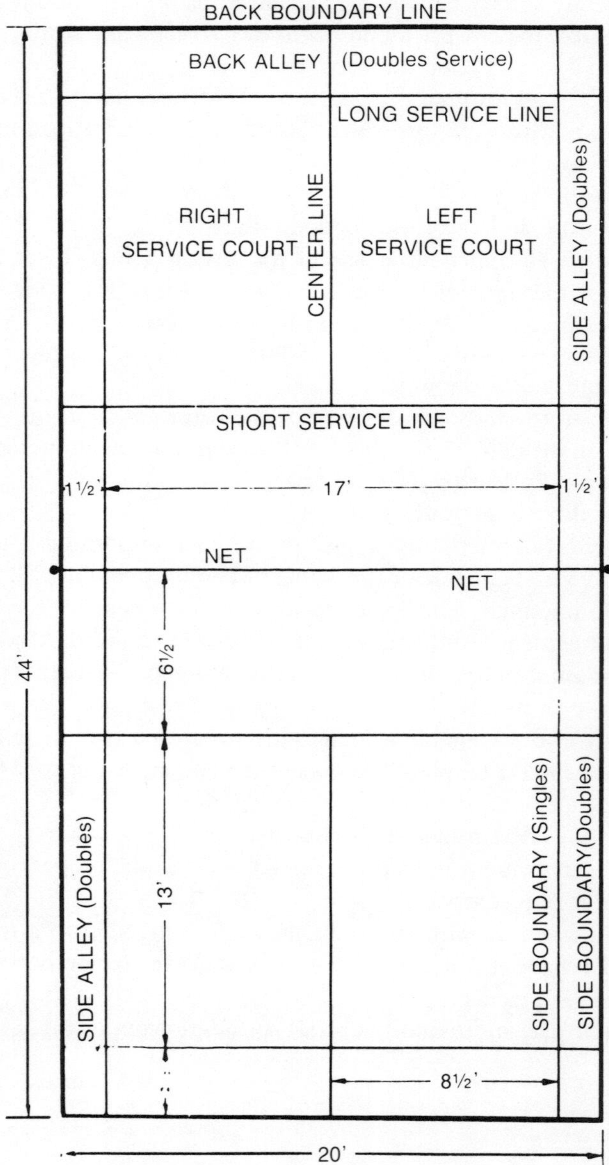

In marking the court, the width 40 mm. (1-1/2 inches) of the center lines shall be equally divided between the right and left service courts; the width 40 mm. each (1-1/2 inches each) of the short service line and the long service line shall fall within the 3.96 meters (13 foot) measurement given as the length of the service court; and the width (1-1/2 inches each) (40 mm. each) of all other boundary lines shall fall within the measurements given.

(b) Where space does not permit of the marking out of a court for doubles, a court may be marked out for singles only as shown in Diagram "B". The back boundary lines become also the long service lines, and the posts, or the strips of materials representing them as referred to in Law 2, shall be placed on the side lines.

Posts

2. The posts shall be 1.55 meters (5 feet 1 inch) in height from the surface of the court. They shall be sufficiently firm to keep the net strained as provided in Law 3, and shall be placed on the side boundary lines of the court. Where this is not practicable, some method must be employed for indicating the position of the side boundary line where it passes under the net, *e.g.*, by the use of a thin post or strips of material, not less than 40 mm. (1-1/2 inches) in width, fixed to the side boundary line and rising vertically to the net cord. Where this is in use on a court marked for doubles it shall be placed on the side boundary line of the doubles court irrespective of whether singles or doubles are being played.

Net

3. The net shall be made of fine natural cord or artificial fiber of a dark color and an even thickness not less than 15 mm. (5/8 inch) and not more than 20 mm. (3/4 inch) mesh. It shall be firmly stretched from post to post, and shall be 0.76 meters (2 feet 6 inches) in depth. The top of the net shall be 1.524 meters (5 feet) in height from the floor at the center, and 1.55 meters (5 feet 1 inch) at the posts, and shall be edged with a 75 mm. (3 inches) white tape doubled and supported by a cord or cable run through the tape and strained over and flush with the top of the posts.

Shuttle

4. (a) **General design**

A shuttle shall have from 14 to 16 feathers fixed in a cork base which is 0.025 to 0.028 meters (1 inch to 1-1/8 inches) in diameter. The feathers shall be from 0.064 to 0.070 meters (2-1/2 to 2-3/4 inches) in length from the tip to the top of the cork base.

The tips of the feathers shall form a circle with a diameter within the range from 0.054 to 0.064 meters (2-1/8 to 2-1/2 inches). The feather shall be fastened firmly with thread or other suitable material. The bottom of the cork shall be rounded and covered by a thin layer of white leather or similar material.

(b) **Weight**

A shuttle shall weigh from 73 to 85 grains (4.75 to 5.50 grams).

(c) **Pace and Flight**

A shuttle shall be deemed to be of correct pace when it is hit by a player with a full underhand stroke from a spot immediately above one back boundary line in a direction parallel to the side lines and at an upward angle, to fall not less than 0.30 meters (one foot) and not more than 0.76 meters (two feet six inches) short of the other back boundary line.

(d) Subject to there being no variation in the general design, weight, pace and flight of the shuttle, modifications in the above specifications may be made, with the approval of the national organization concerned:

i) in places where atmospheric conditions due either to altitude or climate make the standard shuttle unsuitable; or

ii) if special circumstances exist which make it otherwise necessary in the interests of the game.

Players

5. (a) The word "Player applies to all those taking part in a game.
(b) The game shall be played, in the case of the doubles game, by two players a side, and in the case of the singles game, by one player a side.
(c) The side for the time being having the right to serve shall be called the "In" side, and the opposing side shall be called the "Out" side.

The Toss

6. Before commencing play the opposing sides shall toss, and the side winning the toss shall have the option of:—
   (a) Serving first; or
   (b) Not serving first; or
   (c) Choosing ends.
   The side losing the toss shall then have choice of any alternative remaining.

Scoring

7. (a) The doubles and men's singles game consists of 15 points provided that, when the score is 13-all, the side which first reaches 13 has the option of 'setting' the game to 5, and that when the score is 14-all, the side which first reached 14 has the option of 'setting' the game to 3. After a game has been 'set' the score is called 'love all', and the side which first scores 5 or 3 points, according as the game has been 'set' at 13 all or 14 all, wins the game. In either case the claim to 'set' the game must be made before the next service is delivered after the score has reached 13 all or 14 all.
(b) The ladies singles game consists of 11 points. Provided that when the score is "9 all" the player who first reached 9 has the option of "setting" the game to 3, and when the score is "10 all" the player who first reached 10 has the option of "setting" the game to 2.
(c) A side rejecting the option of "setting" at the first opportunity shall not thereby be debarred from "setting" if a second opportunity arises.
(d) Notwithstanding paragraph (a) above, it is permissible by prior arrangement for only one game to be played and also for this to consist of 21 points, in which case "setting" shall be as for the game of 15 points with scores of 19 and 20 being substituted for 13 and 14 respectively.
(e) In handicap games "setting" is not permitted.

8. The opposing sides shall contest the best of three games, unless otherwise agreed. The players shall change ends at the commencement of the second game and also of the third game (if any). In the third game the players shall change ends when the leading score reaches:-
   (a) 8 in a game of 15 points;
   (b) 6 in a game of 11 points;
or, in handicap events, when one of the sides has scored half the total number of points required to win the game (the next highest number being taken in case of fractions). When it has been agreed to play only one game the players shall change ends as provided above for the third game. In a game of 21 points, the players shall change ends when the leading score reaches 11 or in handicap games as indicated above.
   If, inadvertently, the players omit to change ends as provided in this Law at the score indicated, the ends shall be changed immediately the mistake is discovered, and the existing score shall stand.

Doubles Play

9. (a) It having been decided which side is to have the first service, the player in the right-hand service court of that side commences the game by serving to the player in the service court diagonally opposite. If the latter player returns the

shuttle before it touches the ground, it is to be returned by one of the "In" side, and then returned by one of the "Out" side, and so on, till a fault is made or the shuttle ceases to be "in play" (vide paragraph (b)). If a fault is made by the "In" side its right to continue serving is lost, as only one player on the side beginning a game is entitled to do so (vide Law 11), and the opponent in the right-hand service court then becomes the server; but if the service is not returned, or the fault is made by the "Out" side, the "In" side scores a point. The "In" side players then change from one service court to the other, the service now being from the left-hand service court to the player in the service court diagonally opposite. So long as a side remains "in", service is delivered alternately from each service court into the one diagonally opposite, the change being made by the "In" side when, and only when a point is added to its score.
(b) The first service of a side in each innings shall be made from the right-hand service court . A "Service" is delivered as soon as the shuttle is struck by the server's racket. The shuttle is thereafter "in play" until it touches the ground, or until a fault or "let" occurs, or except as provided in Law 19. After the service is delivered the server and the player served to may take up any positions they choose on their side of the net, irrespective of any boundary lines.

10. The player served to may alone receive the service, but should the shuttle touch, or be struck by, his partner the "In" side scores a point. No player may receive two consecutive services in the same game, except as provided in Law 12.

11. Only one player of the side begining a game shall be entitled to serve in its first innings. In all subsequent innings each partner shall have the right, and they shall serve consecutively. The side winning a game shall always serve first in the next game, but either of the winners may serve and either of the losers may receive the service.

12. If a player serves out of turn, or from the wrong service court (owing to a mistake as to the service court from which service is at the time being in order), *and his side wins the rally,* it shall be a "Let", provided that such "Let" be claimed and allowed, or ordered by the umpire, before the next succeeding service is delivered.

If a player of the "Out" side standing in the wrong service court is prepared to receive the service when it is delivered, *and his side wins the rally,* it shall be a "Let", provided that such "Let" be claimed and allowed, or ordered by the umpire, before the next succeeding service is delivered.

If in either of the above cases the side of fault *loses the rally,* the mistake shall stand and the players' positions shall not be corrected.

Should a player inadvertently change sides when he should not do so, and the mistake not be discovered until after the next succeeding service has been delivered, the mistake shall stand and a "Let" cannot be claimed or allowed, and the players' position shall not be corrected.

Singles Play

13. In singles Law 9 to 12 hold good except that:—
    (a) The players shall serve from and receive service in their respective right-hand service courts only when the server's score is 0 or an even number of points in the game, the service being delivered from and received in their respective left-hand service courts when the server's score is an odd number of points. Setting does not affect this sequence.
    (b) Both players shall change service courts after each point has been scored.

Faults

14. A fault made by a player of the side which is "in", puts the server out; if made by a player whose side is "out", it counts a point to the "in" side.

It is a fault:—

(a) If in serving (i) any part of the shuttle at the instant of being struck be higher than the server's waist, or (ii) if at the instant of the shuttle being struck the shaft of the racket be not pointing in a downward direction to such an extent that the whole of the head of the racket is discernibly below the whole of the server's hand holding the racket.

(b) If, in serving, the shuttle does not pass over the net, or falls into the wrong service court *(i.e.,* into the one not diagonally opposite to the server), or falls short of the short service line or beyond the long service line, or outside the side boundary lines of the service court into which service in in order.

(c) If the server's feet are not in the service court from which service is at the time being in order, or if the feet of the player receiving the service are not in the service court diagonally opposite until the service is delivered. (Vide Law 16).

(d) If, once the service has started, any player makes preliminary feints or otherwise intentionally balks his opponent, or if any player deliberately delays serving the shuttle or in getting ready to receive it so as to obtain an unfair advantage. (When the server and receiver have taken up their respective positions to serve and to receive, the first forward movement of the server's racket constitutes the start of the service and such must be continuous thereafter.)

(e) If, either in service or play, the shuttle falls outside the boundaries of the court, or passes through or under the net, or fails to pass the net, or touches the roof or side walls, or the person or dress of a player. (A shuttle falling on a line shall be deemed to have fallen in the court or service court of which such line is a boundary).

*(f) If, when in play, the initial point of contact with the shuttle is not on the striker's side of the net. (The striker may, however, follow the shuttle over the net with his racket in the course of stroke.)

(g) If, when the shuttle is "in play", a player touches the net or its supports with racket, person or dress.

(h) If the shuttle be caught and held on the racket and then slung during the execution of a stroke; or if the shuttle be hit twice in succession by the same player with two strokes; or if the shuttle be hit by a player and his partner successively.

(i) If, in play, a player strikes the shuttle (unless he thereby makes a good return) or is struck by it, whether he is standing within or outside the boundaries of the court.

(j) If a player obstructs an opponent.

(k) If Law 16 be transgressed.

General

15. The server may not serve till his opponent is ready, but the opponent shall be deemed to be ready if a return of the service be attempted.

16. The server and the player served to must stand within the limits of their respective service courts (as bounded by the short and long service, the center, and side lines), and some part of both feet of these players must remain in contact with the surface of the court in a stationary position until the service is delivered. A foot on or touching a line in the case of either the server or the receiver shall be held to be outside his service court (vide Law 14 (c)). The respective partners may take up any position, provided they do not unsight or otherwise obstruct an opponent.

17. (a) If, in the course of service or rally, the shuttle touches and passes over the net, the stroke is not invalidated thereby. It is a good return if the shuttle having passed outside either post drops on or within the boundary lines of the opposite

court. A "Let" may be given by the umpire for any unforeseen or accidental hindrance.

(b) If, in service, or during a rally, a shuttle *after passing over the net,* is caught in or on the net, it is a "Let."

(c) If the receiver is faulted for moving before the service is delivered, or for not being within the correct service court, in accordance with Laws 14 (c) or 16, and at the same time the server is also faulted for a service infringement, it shall be a let.

(d) When a "Let" occurs, the play since the last service shall not count, and the player who served shall serve again, except when Law 12 is applicable.

18. If the server, in attempting to serve, misses the shuttle, it is not a fault; but if the shuttle be touched by the racket, a service is thereby delivered.

19. If, when in play, the shuttle strikes the net and remains suspended there, or strikes the net and falls toward the surface of the court on the striker's side of the net, or hits the surface outside the court and an opponent then touches the net or shuttle with his racket or person, there is no penalty, as the shuttle is not *then* in play.

20. If a player has a chance of striking the shuttle in a downward direction when quite near the net, his opponent must not put up his racket near the net on the chance of the shuttle rebounding from it. This is obstruction within the meaning of Law 14 (j).

A player may, however, hold up his racket to protect his face from being hit if he does not thereby balk his opponent.

21. It shall be the duty of the umpire to call "fault" or "let" should either occur, without appeal being made by the players, and to give his decision on any appeal regarding a point in dispute, if made before the next service; and also to appoint linesmen and service judges at his discretion. The umpire's decision shall be final, but he shall uphold the decision of a linesman or service judge. This shall not preclude the umpire also from faulting the server or receiver. Where, however, a referee is appointed, an appeal shall lie to him from the decision of an umpire on questions of law only.

Continuous Play

22. (a) Play shall be continuous from the first service until the match be concluded; except that:—

(i) in international competitive events there shall be allowed an interval not exceeding five minutes between the second and third games of a match;

(ii) in countries where conditions render it desirable, there shall be allowed, subject to the previously published approval of the national organization concerned, an interval not exceeding five minutes between the second and third games of a match, either singles or doubles or both;

(iii) when necessitated by circumstances not within the control of the players, the umpire may suspend play for such a period as he may consider necessary. If play be suspended the existing score shall stand and play be resumed from that point.

(b) Under no circumstances shall play be suspended to enable a player to recover his strength or wind, or to receive instruction or advice.

(c) Except that in the case of an interval provided for above, without the umpire's consent no player shall be allowed to receive advice during a match or to leave the court until the match be concluded.

(d) The umpire shall be the sole judge of any suspension of play and he shall have the right to disqualify an offender.

NOTE

INTERVALS IN PLAY AS SANCTIONED BY THE I.B.F.

The International competitive events referred to in (a) (i) above are:

(1) The International Badminton Championship (Thomas Cup);
(2) The Ladies' International Badminton Championship (Uber Cup);
(3) The World Championship;
(4) All official international matches;
(5) International Open Championships and other international events of a higher status as sanctioned by the I.B.F.

INTERPRETATIONS

1. Any movement or conduct by the server that has the effect of breaking the continuity of service after the server and receiver have taken their position to serve and to receive the service is a preliminary feint. For example, a server who, after having taken up his position to serve, delays hitting the shuttle for so long as to be unfair to the receiver, is guilty of such conduct.
   (Vide Law 14 (d))
2. It is obstruction if a player invade an opponent's court with racket or person in any degree except as permitted in Law 14 (f)
   (Vide Law 14 (j))
3. Where necessary on account of the structure of a building, the local Badminton Authority may, subject to the right of veto of its National Organization, make by-laws dealing with cases in which a shuttle touches an obstruction.

RECOMMENDATIONS TO UMPIRES

ADOPTED, 1960

(incorporating all amendments subsequently adopted)

1. Thoroughly know "The Laws of Badminton."
2. The umpire's decision is final on all points of fact: a player may, however, appeal to the referee on a point of law only.
3. The lineman's decision is final on all points of fact on his own line: the umpire cannot overrule him. If a linesman is unsighted, the umpire may then give a decision if he can: otherwise a let should be played.
4. Where a service judge is appointed, his decision is final on all points of fact in connection with the delivery of the service as set out in "Service Judge" 27. It shall be the duty of the umpire specially to watch the receiver — see 22 (c).
5. All announcements and calling of the score must be done distinctly and loudly enough to be heard clearly by players and spectators.

   Call promptly and with authority but, if a mistake is made admit it, apologize and correct it.
6. If a decision cannot be given, say so and give a let. NEVER ask spectators nor be influenced by their remarks.
7. The umpire is responsible for all lines not covered by linesmen.
8. The umpire should control the match firmly, but without being officious. He should keep play flowing without unnecessary interruptions while ensuring that the Laws are observed. The game is for the players.
9. When a doubt arises in the mind of the umpire or service judge as to whether an infringement of the Laws has occurred or not, "Fault" should not be called and the game allowed to proceed.

Before Play Begins

10. Obtain the score pad from the referee. Enter up the score pad.
11. Check the net for height. See that the posts are on the lines, or that tapes are correctly placed — Laws 2 and 3.
12. Ensure that the linesmen and service judge are correctly placed and know their job — see "Linesmen" and "Service Judge."
13. Ensure that a sufficient quantity of tested shuttles according to Law 4 is readily available for the match, in order to avoid delays during play. If the players cannot agree, the umpire should have the shuttles tested, or in a tournament refer to the referee, or in a match the captains or referee. Once shuttles have been found to be acceptable, ensure that they are used unless circumstances alter.

Starting the Match

14. Ensure that tossing is correctly carried out, and that the winners and losers exercise correctly their options under Law 6.
15. In the case of doubles, mark on the score pad the names of the players starting in the right-hand service courts. This enables a check to be made at any time to see if the players are in their correct service courts. If during the game the players get in their wrong service courts unnoticed, so that they have to stay wrong — Law 12 — amend the score pad accordingly.
16. When the players have finished warming-up announce:—
    (a) In a Tournament:—
        1. "Final or semi-final of . . . ." If neither, say nothing.
    (b) In a tournament or match:—
        1. Names of players with country, county or club where applicable
        2. Name of the first server, and, in the case of doubles, of the receiver.
        3. To start a match, call "Love all, play."

The Match

17. Mark the score pad as the match proceeds.
18. Call the score:—
    (a) Always call the server's score first.
    (b) Singles — when a player loses his service, call "Service over" followed by the score in favor of the new server.
    (c) Doubles — at the beginning of a game call the score only, and continue to do so as long as the first player serves. When the right to serve is lost call "Service over" followed by the score in favor of the new server. In that and subsequent innings when the first server loses his right to serve, call the score followed by "Second server." Continue this as long as the second player serves. When a side loses the right to serve call "Service over" followed by the score in favor of the new server.
    (d) When a side reaches 14, or in the case of ladies' singles 10, call on the first occasion only "Game point" or "Match point." If a further game or match point occurs after setting, call it again on the first occasion. "Game point" or "Match point" should always immediately follow the server's score where applicable, and precede the receiver's score.
    (e) When the shuttle falls outside a line for which the umpire is responsible in the absence of a linesman, call "Out" before calling the score.
19 See that no unnecessary delay occurs, or that the players do not leave the court without permission of the umpire — Law 22.
20. If an unavoidable hold-up occurs in a match, record the score, server and the correct service courts of the players on the score pad.
21. If a shuttle or other object not connected with the match in progress invades the court or its environs, "Let" should be called.
22. Look for:—
    (a) Faulty serving if there is no service judge. It is difficult to detect from the chair

"Serving above the waist", or "racket head above the hand." If there is any doubt, caution the player and ask for a service judge.

(b) The server having both feet on the floor in a stationary position INSIDE the service court when the shuttle is struck, and that there is no feint — Law 14(d) and Interpretation 1. This should be the responsibility of the service judge if available. Where the official responsible considers that there has been a flagrant fault under Law 14(d), as described in Interpretation 1, he shall fault the server as soon as the service is delivered. However, each case should be judged on its merits and, if it is considered that the server tends to delay too long, the umpire should, either on his responsibility, or at the request of the service judge, warn the player that he will be faulted should he continue to delay. (See also Recommendation 33).

(c) The receiver having both feet on the floor in a stationary position INSIDE the service court until the service is delivered, and that he does not move before the shuttle is struck — Laws 14(c) and 16.

(d) Strokes which are faults under Law 14 (h). These should be immediately called by the umpire as "Fault".

(e) On no account allow players to call 'no shot,' fault,' etc. Warn them if they do, as it may distract their opponents.

(f) Obstruction — for instance, sliding under the net; throwing the racket into the opponent's court; balking, unsighting an opponent during service. See Laws 14(d), 14(j), 16, 20 and Interpretation 2.

(g) Serving and receiving out of turn or in the wrong court. Law 12 should be thoroughly understood.

(h) Striking the shuttle before it crosses the net, and hitting the net with racket, person or dress, while the shuttle is in play — Laws 14(f) and 14(g).

(i) The option of "setting" being correctly exercised — Law 7. It is the duty of the umpire to ask the player's or players' decision. Announce the decision loudly so that spectators can hear, calling "Set 2 points" (or 3 or 5 as appropriate) followed by "Love all" or "Love all, second server," as the case may be.

(j) The players changing ends at the correct score in the third game — Law 8.

(k) A player interfering with the correct speed of a shuttle. The player should be warned, and the shuttle discarded if necessary.

The End of a Game

23. Announce: — "Game to . . . ." (the name(s) of the player(s) in a tournament or the name of the team represented in the case of a meeting of representative teams) followed by the score and, if appropriate, by "One game all".

In the case of a match in a meeting between two teams, always define the contestants by the name of the team represented and not by the names of the actual players.

The End of the match

24. Announce the result and score.
25. Immediately take the completed and signed score pad to the referee in a tournament, or to the captains in a match.

Service judge

26. If only one is appointed, he should sit on a low chair by the net post preferably opposite the umpire, but on the same side as the umpire if circumstances so dictate. If two are appointed, each should sit on a low chair behind the back boundary line, or in accordance with the direction of the umpire.
27. The service judge, where only one is appointed, or the service judge on the server's side of the court when two are appointed, is responsible for seeing that the server:—

(a) until the shuttle is s truck, has some part of both feet in a stationary position on the floor INSIDE the service court — Law 16 and Recommendation 32 — and does not feint — Law 14(d) and Interpretation 1.

(b) at the moment of striking the shuttle does not have ANY part of the racket above ANY part of the hand holding the racket — Law 14 (a) (see Diagram) and does not have any part of the shuttle above his waist — Law 14(a).

LAW 14 — DELIVERY OF SERVICE

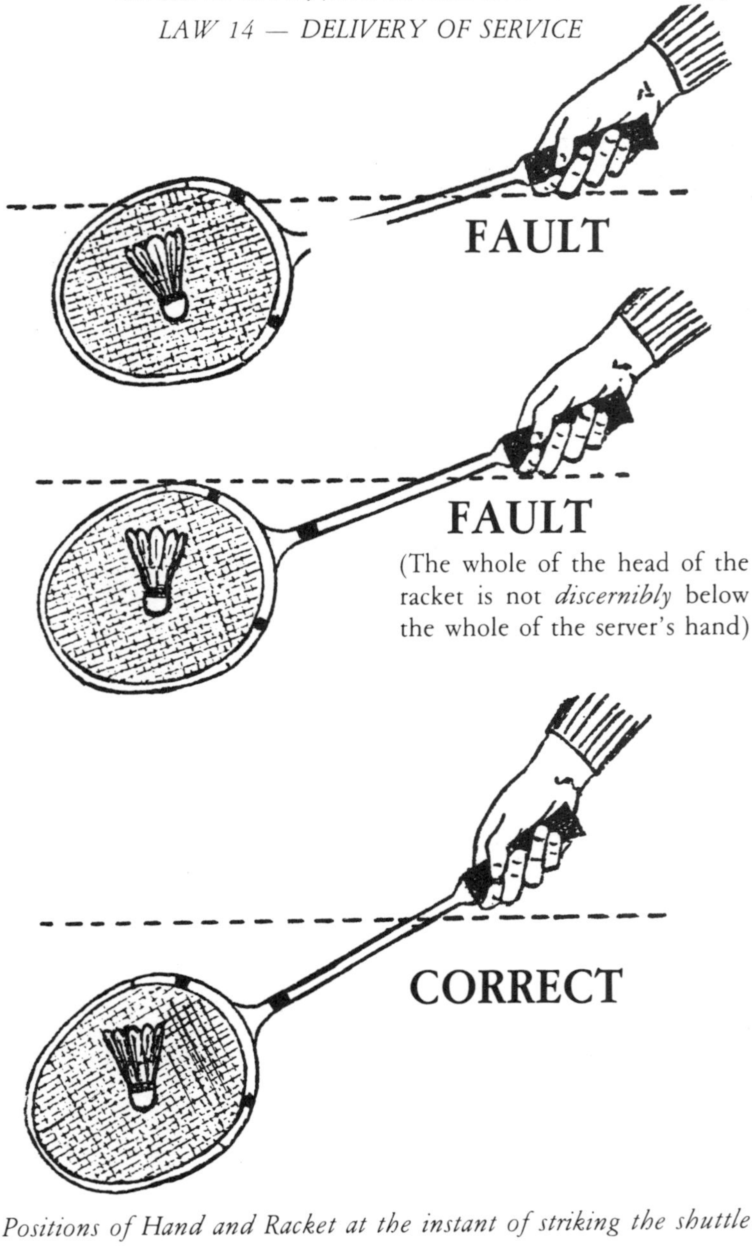

Positions of Hand and Racket at the instant of striking the shuttle.

28. If the server does not comply with all of 27 the service judge responsible should immediately call "Fault" loudly and ensure that the umpire hears him.

Where two service judges are appointed the one on the receiver's side should be made responsible for calling "Fault" for infringement of Law 16 on the part of the receiver. He should call "Fault" loudly and ensure that the umpire hears him.

In addition this shall not preclude the umpire also from faulting the server or receiver.

The umpire may arrange with the service judge, or judges, any extra duties which he wishes either to undertake, provide that the players are so advised.

Linesmen

*29. A linesman is entirely responsible for his line. If the shuttle falls out, no matter how far, call "Out" promptly in a clear voice loud enough to be heard by the players and the spectators, and at the same time signal by extending both arms horizontally so that the umpire can see clearly. If the shuttle falls in, the linesman shall say nothing, but point to the line with his right hand. If unsighted, he shall inform the umpire immediately by putting both hands up crossed to cover his eyes.

30. Linesmen should be sited on chairs in prolongation of their lines, at the ends of the court and at the side opposite to the umpire.

31. If three linesmen are available, two should take a back boundary line and (in doubles) long service line each, the third the sideline furthest from the umpire.

If further linesmen are available, they should be used according to the umpire's preference.

Interpretations

32. It is not a fault under Law 16 if either the server of the receiver raises any part of either or both feet, provided that some part of both feet does maintain contact with the same part of the surface of the court.

*33. It is not a fault under Law 16 if the server, after having taken up his position to serve, should then take one step forward before striking the shuttle, always provided that he had not started to swing his racket forward before taking such step.

Glossary of Terms

A.B.A.: American Badminton Association, governing body in the U.S. (name changed to U.S. Badminton Association in 1977)

Ace: A serve which is not hit by the opponent and the shuttle lands in the serve returners court, scoring a point for the server.

Alley: The 1½ foot increase in width on each side of the singles court to comprise the additional size of the doubles court.

Attacking Clear: (Offensive clear). Low, flat clear used to run your opponent to his baseline (back boundary line).

Backcourt: Area between the center and back boundary of the court.

Backhand: Strokes hit on the opposite side of the body from the racket hand (left side of body for right-handed players).

Base: Central position to which the player tries to return after each shot.

Baseline: Back boundary line of court.

Bird: Slang term for shuttlecock or shuttle. The object hit back and forth over the net.

Block Shot: A net shot using very little racket movement to return a smash or drive primarily from the rebound of the speed of the oncoming shuttle.

Carry: (sling, throw). A shot in which the shuttle slides on the racket and is returned at a low speed, misdirected for the intended shot. A carry was illegal until 1981. This shot is now allowed if hit unintentionally.

Clear: (Lob). A shot hit high and deep to the opponent's backcourt.

Court: Area marked by boundary lines for playing badminton.

Cross-court: A shot hit diagonally from one side of the court to the other.

Cut Shot: (Slice). A shot in which the racket brushes across the shuttle at an angle to the direction of the swing in order to reduce the speed of the flight and change the direction of the flight of the shuttle.

Deception: Body movement or racket movement which is intended to lead the receiver to believe the shuttle will be hit at a different speed or in a different direction than the actual shot.

Defense: Situation you are in when your opponent has the opportunity to hit a smash.

Double Hit: Hitting the shuttle twice in succession during the same shot or if in doubles both players touch the shuttle in hitting the return. It is a fault.

Drive: A side arm stroke hit low and flat to land between the opponent's short service line and back boundary line.

Drive Serve: A hard and quickly hit service with a flat trajectory.

Drop Shot: A shot hit from any place in the court which passes close to the net and lands in your opponent's court between the net and short service line.

Even Court: The side of the court corresponding with the right service court.

Face: Strung surface of racket.

Fault: Violation of the rules. See Rule 14.

First server: A term in doubles to indicate that both players still have the opportunity to serve in that inning.

Flick: A shot hit from the player's forecourt which just passes by or over the opponent's outstretched racket into his backcourt.

Flick Serve: A service hit with a trajectory to just pass over the opponent's outstretched racket and land near the long service line.

Follow-through: Movement of racket and body after racket contacts shuttle during the execution of any shot.

Footwork: Technique of positioning feet in moving about the court.

Foot Fault: A violation of the rules as the result of the position and/or movement of the server or service returner's feet.

Forecourt: Area between the net and the center of the court (short service line).

Forehand: Strokes hit on the right side of the body for a right-handed player, and left side for a left-handed player.

Game: The games consists of 15 points for men's singles and all doubles matches, and 11 points in ladies' singles, unless the game has been set (See Rule 7; Scoring).

Game Bird: Rally which, if won by the server, results in his winning the game.

Hairpin Net Shot: A re-drop in which the shuttle is hit just barely over the top of the net and falls close to the net taking a flight pattern resembling the shape of a hairpin.

Hand in: See first server.

Hand Out: See second server.

I.B.F.: International Badminton Federation, a world-governing body founded in 1934.

Inning: Period during which a player or team holds the service.

Kill: A smash hit to end the rally. A winner or put-away.

Let: An incident which requires the replay of a rally (See Rules 12 and 17).

Love: A term used to indicate a score of 0.

Love-All: A term used at the beginning of a match to indicate a score of 0-0 or when the game has been set.

Lob: See Clear.

Match: The best two out of three games.

Match Point: The rally which, if won by the server, wins the match.
Midcourt: The middle area of the court, about halfway between the net and back boundary line.
Mixed Doubles: A match contested between a male and female on each team.
Net Shot: A shot played to the opponent's forecourt, dropping sharply near the net.
Net Tape: White strip demarking the top of the net.
No Shot: Expression sometimes used when calling a fault.
Obstruction: Player blocking the view of the (unsighted) serve returner (female playing forecourt during service in mixed doubles) or player interfering with opponent's execution of a shot near the net.
Odd Court: The side of the court corresponding with the left service court.
Offense: When you are on the attack or have the opportunity to hit a smash.
Off-speed Shot: See Cut Shot.
Overhead: Strokes hit above head height.
Passing Shot: A shot in which the shuttle goes past the opponent at his side.
Point: Unit of scoring.
Power Shot: Overhead smash or clear.
Put-away: See Kill
Racket: Implement used to strike the shuttle.
Rally: The exchange of shots during play. Term used meaning to warm up by hitting the shuttle back and forth.
Ready Position: See Base.
Receiver: Player who receives the service.
Round-the-head Shot: An overhead shot hit from the backhand side of the body using the forehand stroking pattern.
Rush-the-service: Quick movement and shot by the receiver to gain the attack on the return of service primarily used in doubles and mixed doubles.
Second Server: Term used in doubles to indicate one player has lost his service (or is "down") and his partner has his service.
Service: Act of putting the shuttle into play, beginning the rally.
Server: Player who hits the serve.
Service Court: (Receiver's court). Area into which the serve must be delivered.
Service Over: Term indicating the other player of team gains the service.
Setting: Method of extending the game when the score is tied near the end of the game (see Rule 7).

Set-up: A shot which will generally allow the opponent to hit a kill or winner.

Shot: A clear, smash, drive or drop that has been hit from one of the stroking positions.

Shuttlecock:(Shuttle, Bird). The object hit back and forth over the net constructed of cork and feathers or synthetic (nylon or plastics).

Side-by-side Formation: Defensive doubles positioning. Each player defends his side of the court.

Sling: See Carry (Throw)

Smash: The hard overhead shot hit at a steep angle. It is the basic offensive shot to win the rally.

Speed Line: The line between the player's base position and the point at which he will strike the shuttle. Efficient movement patterns orient the body along this line when the player moves to hit the shuttle.

Stroke: Basic hitting patterns from which all shots are executed. They include overhead, side arm, and underhand strokes on both the forehand and backhand side of the body and strokes hit from in front of the body.

Thomas Cup: International Men's team competition held every three years.

Trajectory: Angle of the shuttle's flight.

Uber Cup: International Women's team competition held every three years.

Underhand: Stroke in which the shuttle is generally contacted below waist level.

Up-and-back Formation: Basic attack or offensive formation in doubles and predominant positioning for mixed doubles with female playing forecourt.

U.S.B.A.: U.S. Badminton Association, formed in 1977 when ABA was dissolved.

Wood Shot: When base of shuttle strikes the frame of the racket. This is no longer a fault.

W.B.F.: World Badminton Federation, a world-governing body founded in 1977.

Winner: See Kill (Put-away).

BIBLIOGRAPHY

Books

Bloss, Margaret Varner. **Badminton,** 2nd Edition, Wm. C. Brown Co., Dubuque, Iowa, 1971.

Brown, Edward. **The Complete Book of Badminton,** Stackpole Books, Harrisburg, Pa., 1969.

Davidson, Kenneth, and Leland Gustavson. **Winning Badminton,** The Ronald Press Co., New York, 1953.

Davis, Pat. **Badminton Complete,** A.S. Barnes and Co., Cranbury, N.J., 1967.

Devlin, J. Frank, and Rex Lardner (Eds.). **Sports Illustrated Book of Badminton,** J.E. Lippincott Co., N.Y., 1967.

Finston, Irv, and Charles Remsberg. **Inside Badminton,** Contemporary Books, Chicago, Ill., 1978.

Mills Roger. **Badminton,** E.P. Publishing Ltd., Great Britain, 1977.

Poole, James. **Badminton,** 2nd Ed., Goodyear Publishing Co., Santa Monica, CA, 1973.

Rogers, Winn. **Advanced Badminton,** Wm. C. Brown Co., Dubuque, Iowa, 1971.

Rutledge, Abbie, and John Friedrich. **Beginning Badminton,** Wadsworth Publishing Co., Inc., Belmont, Ca., 1969.

Whetnall, Paul and Sue Whetnall, **Badminton**, Pelham Books, London, 1975.

Magazines and Guides

Badminton Gazette, Official publication of the Badminton Assoc., of England, 81a High Street, Bromley, Kent, England.

Badminton, U.S.A., Official publication of the U.S. Badminton Assoc., P.O. Box 237, Swartz Creek, MI. 48473

World Badminton, Official Publication of the International Badminton Federation, SBU Office, Cockburn Center, 40 Bogmoor Place, Glasgow G514TQ, Scotland.

NAGWS Guide: Badminton-Squash-Racquetball. American Alliance for Health, Physical Education, Recreation, and Dance, 1900 Association Dr., Reston, VA 22091.

Films

The Athletic Institute, 200 Castlewood Drive, North Palm Beach, FL 33408 (in 16mm, 8mm, and video)

Grip, Footwork, Serves
Basic Strokes
Basic Strategy and Drills

USBA Film Library, USBA, P.O. Box 237, Swartz Creek, MI.48473 (Film rental)

— DISCOUNT COUPON —

Take advantage of our 50th anniversary offer. Purchase any of the following titles at a $1.00 discount.

Sports Technique Series: Self-teaching books providing authoritative personal perspectives on how to increase skills and knowledge in various athletic disciplines.

- ☐ Archery
- ☐ Badminton
- ☐ Championship Baseball
- ☐ Better Basketball
- ☐ Basketball: Woman's Game
- ☐ Modern Women's Gymnastics
- ☐ On the Lesson Tee
- ☐ Pathfinder (Backpacking)
- ☐ Power Volleyball: Women's Game
- ☐ Raquetball 1-2-3
- ☐ Softball: Fast & Slow Pitch
- ☐ Tennis Your Way
- ☐ Track & Field
- ☐ Women's Self-Defense

Youth League Series: Definitive sources of basic information on team sports. Excellent resource for the youth league coach and player. Covers fundamental techniques, strategies, tactics and rules.

☐ Baseball ☐ Basketball ☐ Football ☐ Soccer ☐ Softball

List price $6.95. Your price $5.95. Add $1.25 for first book, 50¢ for each additional title to cover shipping and handling. Florida residents add 5% sales tax. Check, money order, Visa and MC accepted.

Name ______________________________

Address ______________________________

City and State ____________________ Zip __________

VISA/M.C. # ______________________________

Expiration Date ______________________________

Mail to: **ATHLETIC INSTITUTE (Publication Department)**
200 Castlewood Drive, North Palm Beach, FL 33408